DISEASES &
DISORDERS

Lou
Gehrig's
Disease

Titles in the Diseases and Disorders series include:

Lou Gehrig's Disease

Melissa Abramovitz

LUCENT BOOKS

An imprint of Thomson Gale, a part of The Thomson Corporation

THOMSON
★
GALE

Detroit • New York • San Francisco • San Diego • New Haven, Conn.
Waterville, Maine • London • Munich

LIBRARY OF CONGRESS CATALOGING-IN-PUBLICATION DATA

Abramovitz, Melissa, 1954–
  Lou Gehrig's Disease / by Melissa Abramovitz.
    p. cm. — (Diseases and disorders)
  Includes bibliographical references and index.
    ISBN 1-59018-676-1 (hard cover : alk. paper) 1. Gehrig, Lou, 1903–1941—Juvenile literature. 2. Amyotrophic lateral sclerosis—Juvenile literature. I. Title. II. Series: Diseases and disorders series.
  RC406.A24A37 2006
  616.8'39—dc22

                                                                    2005022650

Table of Contents

"The Most Difficult Puzzles Ever Devised"

Charles Best, one of the pioneers in the search for a cure for diabetes, once explained what it is about medical research that intrigued him so. "It's not just the gratification of knowing one is helping people," he confided, "although that probably is a more heroic and selfless motivation. Those feelings may enter in, but truly, what I find best is the feeling of going toe to toe with nature, of trying to solve the most difficult puzzles ever devised. The answers are there somewhere, those keys that will solve the puzzle and make the patient well. But how will those keys be found?"

Since the dawn of civilization, nothing has so puzzled people—and often frightened them, as well—as the onset of illness in a body or mind that had seemed healthy before. A seizure, the inability of a heart to pump, the sudden deterioration of muscle tone in a small child—being unable to reverse such conditions or even to understand why they occur was unspeakably frustrating to healers. Even before there were names for such conditions, even before they were understood at all, each was a reminder of how complex the human body was, and how vulnerable.

While our grappling with understanding diseases has been frustrating at times, it has also provided some of humankind's most heroic accomplishments. Alexander Fleming's accidental discovery in 1928 of a mold that could be turned into penicillin has resulted in the saving of untold millions of lives. The isolation of the enzyme insulin has reversed what was once a death sentence for anyone with diabetes. There have been great strides in combating conditions for which there is not yet a cure, too. Medicines can help AIDS patients live longer, diagnostic tools such as mammography and ultrasounds can help doctors find tumors while they are treatable, and laser surgery techniques have made the most intricate, minute operations routine.

This "toe-to-toe" competition with diseases and disorders is even more remarkable when seen in a historical continuum. An astonishing amount of progress has been made in a very short time. Just two hundred years ago, the existence of germs as a cause of some diseases was unknown. In fact, it was less than 150 years ago that a British surgeon named Joseph Lister had difficulty persuading his fellow doctors that washing their hands before delivering a baby might increase the chances of a healthy delivery (especially if they had just attended to a diseased patient)!

Each book in Lucent's Diseases and Disorders series explores a disease or disorder and the knowledge that has been accumulated (or discarded) by doctors through the years. Each book also examines the tools used for pinpointing a diagnosis, as well as the various means that are used to treat or cure a disease. Finally, new ideas are presented—techniques or medicines that may be on the horizon.

Frustration and disappointment are still part of medicine, for not every disease or condition can be cured or prevented. But the limitations of knowledge are being pushed outward constantly; the "most difficult puzzles ever devised" are finding challengers every day.

Who Was Lou Gehrig?

Lou Gehrig was born on June 19, 1903, in New York City to German immigrants. His family was poor but valued education, and Lou was encouraged to go to college. He went to Columbia University on a football scholarship and also played baseball for the university. His baseball hitting skills impressed a scout for the New York Yankees, who signed him to the team in 1923 with a fifteen-hundred-dollar bonus.

Gehrig began playing first base in 1925 and did not miss a game for thirteen years. His record of 2,130 consecutive games was not broken until 1995 by Cal Ripken Jr. Gehrig played through broken bones and back spasms. His endurance and strength earned him the nickname "Iron Horse."

In 1927 Gehrig hit more home runs than anyone except teammate Babe Ruth and was named the team's most valuable player. In 1932 Gehrig became the first player in the American League to hit four home runs in a game. Despite Gehrig and Ruth's dominance as hitters, however, the two had an argument during an off-season overseas trip and did not speak to each other for six years.

Gehrig won the Triple Crown in 1934 and was named the most valuable player again in 1936, when he led his league in home runs and runs scored. But in 1938 Gehrig's batting average began to fall. His strength seemed depleted. He stopped hitting home runs. Doctors diagnosed a gall bladder problem and put him on a bland diet, but he grew weaker. He managed only four hits during the first eight games of the 1939 season, and after he had trouble getting to first base after one hit, he took himself out of the game.

Gehrig went to the Mayo Clinic in Minnesota to see specialists and was diagnosed with a rare degenerative disease called amyotrophic lateral sclerosis (ALS). His baseball career was over.

On July 4, 1939, the Yankees held a special recognition day for Lou Gehrig. In front of more than sixty-two thousand fans at Yankee Stadium, Gehrig said:

> Fans, for the past two weeks you have been reading about the
> bad break I got. Yet today I consider myself the luckiest man on

Baseball great Lou Gehrig, the most famous American victim of ALS, is honored in Yankee Stadium on July 4, 1939.

Lou Gehrig wipes tears away in response to the ovation given to him by the Yankee faithful after his farewell speech. Considered the greatest speech in baseball history, it made the world aware of ALS.

the face of this earth. I have been in ballparks for seventeen years and have never received anything but kindness and encouragement from you fans.

Look at these grand men. Which of you wouldn't consider it the highlight of his career just to associate with them for even one day? Sure, I'm lucky. Who wouldn't consider it an honor to have known Jacob Ruppert? Also, the builder of baseball's greatest empire, Ed Barrow? To have spent six years with that wonderful little fellow Miller Huggins? Then to have spent the next nine years with that outstanding leader, that smart student of psychology, the best manager in baseball today, Joe McCarthy? Sure, I'm lucky.

When the New York Giants, a team you would give your right arm to beat, and vice versa, sends you a gift—that's something. When everybody down to the groundskeepers and those boys in white coats [physicians] remember you with trophies—that's something. When you have a wonderful mother-in-law who takes sides with you in squabbles with her own daughter—that's something. When you have a father and a mother who work all their lives so you can have an education and build your body—it's a blessing. When you have a wife who has been a tower of strength and shown more courage than you dreamed existed—that's the finest I know.

So I close in saying that I may have had a tough break, but I have an awful lot to live for.[1]

According to the Lou Gehrig Official Web Site, "It was one of the most poignant and emotional moments in the history of American sports, and there was not a dry eye in Yankee Stadium. At the close of Gehrig's speech, Babe Ruth walked up, put his arm around his former teammate and spoke in his ear the first words they had shared since 1934."[2]

Lou Gehrig was elected to the National Baseball Hall of Fame that same year. Although his health was failing rapidly, he participated in community work helping troubled youth until he was no longer able. When he died from ALS on June 2, 1941, he was remembered not only as a baseball powerhouse but also as a kind and honest person. Amytrophic lateral sclerosis became known as Lou Gehrig's disease in his memory, and it retains that name today in the United States.

CHAPTER ONE

What Is Lou Gehrig's Disease?

Amyotrophic lateral sclerosis is referred to as Lou Gehrig's disease or ALS in the United States, but in England it is known as motor neuron disease, and in some parts of the world it is called Charcot's disease after Jean-Martin Charcot. Charcot was a French physician who, in 1874, wrote the first thorough description of the clinical and biological characteristics of ALS. His observations of the disease were extremely accurate and are still studied in modern medicine.

Although ALS is most closely associated with Lou Gehrig in the United States, the disease has also affected other famous people, including Hall of Fame pitcher Jim "Catfish" Hunter, Senator Jacob Javits, actors Michael Zaslow and David Niven, Sesame Street creator Jon Stone, boxer Ezzard Charles, basketball player George Yardley, football player Glenn Montgomery, and musician Leadbelly (Huddie Ledbetter).

Amyotrophic Lateral Sclerosis

The word *amyotrophic* comes from the Greek words *a*, meaning "no" or "negative"; *myo*, meaning "muscle"; *trophic*, meaning "nourishment;" so *amyotrophic* means "no muscle nourishment." *Lateral* refers to the areas in the spinal cord where portions of the nerve cells that signal and control muscles are located. *Sclerosis* means "scarring" or "hardening."

Taken together, the three words mean that scarring in the nerve cells that provide instructions to muscles keeps these muscles from functioning properly.

The name *amyotrophic lateral sclerosis* reveals the nature of the disease as one in which nerve cells, or neurons, are destroyed. The brain and spinal cord have billions of neurons, and different types of neurons are responsible for different functions. The cells affected in ALS are the motor neurons, which control the skeletal muscles. Both upper motor neurons, found in the brain and brain stem (the area that connects the brain and spinal cord), and lower motor neurons, found in the brain stem and spinal cord, are damaged in ALS. As these cells degenerate,

British physicist Stephen Hawking is one of the best-known people afflicted with ALS.

they can no longer send impulses to the muscle fibers that control movement, and the muscles begin to waste away, or atrophy.

This disorder affects one to two of every one hundred thousand adults worldwide, spanning cultures, climates, geography, and races. In the United States, more than fifty-six hundred people are diagnosed each year with Lou Gehrig's disease. The ALS Association estimates that about thirty thousand people have the disease in this country at any given time. Sixty percent of these people are male, and 93 percent are Caucasian. Most affected people are between forty and seventy years old, though the disease has been reported in young adults and even in children.

Although the usual number of affected people is fairly consistent worldwide, there have been several so-called clusters of ALS noted by experts in various places throughout the world. One area during the first half of the twentieth century

Jean-Martin Charcot

Jean-Martin Charcot was born in Paris, France, on November 29, 1825. As a child he developed an interest in medicine as well as in drawing and painting. He decided on a career as a physician and went to work at the renowned Salpêtriére Hospital. At the age of thirty-seven he was appointed senior physician at the hospital. Charcot's work in neurology led to the institution's prominence in this field, and the doctor himself became known as a great teacher and clinician. Charcot also became a professor of pathological anatomy at the University of Paris in 1872, and in 1882 he was appointed as the first chairman of its department of neurology.

Charcot is known in particular for his work that correlated a patient's symptoms with lesions or other abnormalities of the nervous system seen at autopsy. He studied many diseases in this manner, and his work is still considered to be accurate in many areas. His work on the pathology of the liver, kidneys, heart, and lungs also brought him fame. But his main focus was always on where the rate of ALS was fifty to one hundred times more prevalent than in the rest of the world was the western Pacific Ocean. Affected were Japanese people in the Kii peninsula of Honshu Island, the Chamorro people on the island of Guam, the Rota of Micronesia, and the Auyu and Jakai people of West New Guinea. However, during the second half of the twentieth century the ALS rates among these populations declined and are now similar to those elsewhere. The reasons for both the previous higher rates and for the decline are unknown.

What Are the Symptoms of ALS?

Although ALS is relatively rare, its symptoms are dramatic and devastating. The first references to symptoms began to appear in medical writings in the 1830s in England and France. One early description of the disease was written in 1853 by the

neurology, and in addition to being the first to write a formal description of ALS, he is known for his descriptions of several other diseases of the nervous system.

Besides his contributions to medicine, Jean-Martin Charcot was an accomplished artist and an animal lover who avoided animal experimentation and loathed the idea of hunting for sport. He be-

gan to experience ill health in 1890 and died three years later from pulmonary edema, a condition in which the lungs fill with fluid.

French scientist Jean-Martin Charcot was the first to formally describe amyotrophic lateral sclerosis (ALS).

French physician Leon Jean Baptiste Cruveilhier, who reported on the case of Prosper Lecomte, a circus proprietor. The thirty-year-old Lecomte's first symptom was weakness of the right hand. This was followed several months later by weakness in both legs. Then Lecomte experienced weakness of the left hand and slurred speech, followed by progressive weakness and disability throughout his body. He became bedridden and unable to speak or swallow; he died at age thirty-five.

Most cases of Lou Gehrig's disease start with a stage in which motor neurons begin to degenerate but no symptoms are apparent. The length of this phase can vary, depending on how fast the motor neurons become diseased and unable to function. By the time a patient begins to notice symptoms such as muscle weakness, 80 percent of the motor neurons in the spinal cord may already be lost.

Muscle weakness in a hand, arm, leg, or foot or in the muscles that control speech or swallowing is generally the first indication of ALS. As explained in the book *Amyotrophic Lateral Sclerosis*, edited by Hiroshi Mitsumoto and Theodore L. Munsat:

> Muscle weakness is the cardinal sign and symptom of ALS. It almost always occurs in isolated muscle areas at onset and is followed by progressive weakness. Weakness in ALS is not usually associated with pain. Muscle weakness in the hand muscles causes difficulty in performing fine movements with the fingers, such as pinching, turning keys, buttoning, using a zipper, or writing. When it occurs in the arms, people may be unable to carry an object, throw a ball, or raise an object above shoulder level. When weakness develops in the foot, the foot commonly slaps the floor. Such "foot drop" makes climbing stairs difficult, and patients may trip and fall.[3]

Some patients experience weakness in more than one area at the onset of the disease, but usually symptoms begin with one affected area. Other rarely occurring first indications of ALS are weakness in muscles at the back of the neck or breath-

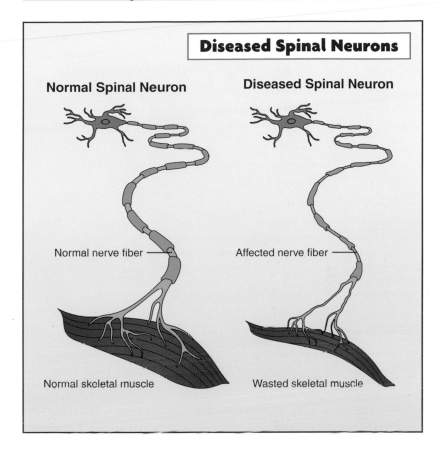

Diseased Spinal Neurons

Normal Spinal Neuron

Diseased Spinal Neuron

Normal nerve fiber

Affected nerve fiber

Normal skeletal muscle

Wasted skeletal muscle

ing difficulties due to degeneration of the muscles that control respiration. Additional rare early symptoms are muscle twitching and weight loss.

Many patients experience muscle cramps early on in the disease. Some have muscle stiffness and fatigue. Most go on to experience a loss of dexterity that means movements become slow and clumsy. Muscles also become spastic; that is, when the muscle is stretched or shortened during movement, this triggers a reflex that delays muscle relaxation. This means that the muscle may become locked in place and extremely difficult to move.

Another typical symptom of early ALS is that muscles have an exaggerated stretch reflex. This means that when a doctor tests reflexes by tapping an area such as the knee with a special hammer, the patient's reflexive response is greater than

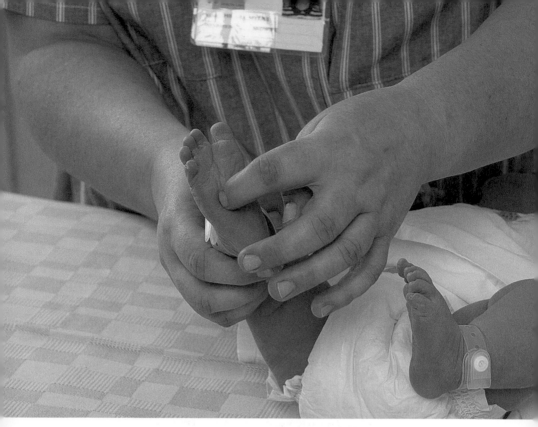

An early indicator of ALS is the Babinski sign, in which the big toe extends upward and the other toes fan out in response to touch.

normal and may also spread to adjacent muscles. Patients also usually display the Babinski sign, in which the big toe extends upward and the other toes fan out in response to having the outer edge of the sole stroked with a blunt object from the heel to the toes. This is one test that a neurologist, or doctor who is an expert on the nervous system, performs when trying to determine whether a patient has Lou Gehrig's disease.

Symptoms as the Disease Progresses

When the disease affects speaking, chewing, and swallowing, these activities become impaired and very slow and stiff. The muscles involved in producing sound and speech become weak, leading to an inability to shout or sing and a weakened voice. The voice may become whispery or hoarse and enunciation becomes difficult. Many patients become unable to speak at all. This can be extremely distressing. According to the Muscular Dystrophy Association, a support organization for neuromuscular diseases including ALS, "For many people with ALS, the loss of mobility and strength is less devastating than the loss of the ability to speak."[4]

Swallowing both solid food and liquids also becomes difficult. Many patients cannot manipulate food inside the mouth or push food into the throat. Liquids may regurgitate into the nose if the valve between the mouth and nose does not close properly. When food or liquid does get past the throat, it may enter the airway rather than the esophagus. This can be life-threatening if the substance cannot be coughed up. Many patients also experience drooling because they can no longer swallow saliva.

Weakness in the respiratory muscles and the diaphragm are also frequent symptoms in Lou Gehrig's disease as the condition progresses. Breathing becomes increasingly difficult, especially when the patient is lying down. In rare cases respiration becomes disabled early on in the disease, but this usually does not occur until later on in the course of ALS. In fact, breathing difficulties are the most frequent cause of death among ALS sufferers.

Another typical symptom of ALS is poor control of emotional behaviors, leading to instances in which the patient suddenly starts laughing or crying. This is due to the death of certain neurons in the centers of the brain that control such behaviors.

As Lou Gehrig's disease progresses, most patients begin to lose weight because of muscle wasting and difficulty eating. Some lose large amounts of weight from a condition called ALS cachexia, in which fat beneath the skin and in the abdominal cavity disappears.

General fatigue is another common symptom. Some muscular deformities are also characteristic of the disease. For example, some patients experience stiffness in the lower legs that results in a shortening of the Achilles tendon. Some develop claw hand, in which the hand assumes the posture of a claw due to weakness of certain muscles and tightness of the joints. Weakening of the muscles can also cause loosening of the joint between the shoulder and the arm, which makes the arm sag from the shoulder joint.

Another common symptom of ALS is acid reflux, in which acid regurgitates from the stomach into the esophagus due to weakened diaphragm muscles. This may lead to heartburn, throat irritation, nausea, chest pain, and insomnia.

In late stages of the disease, ALS sometimes affects sensory and cognitive functions as well as motor functions. Some patients experience burning, prickling sensations on the skin and show some abnormal results on certain laboratory tests of skin sensation. Some become confused or forgetful, which can be a sign of either depression or, more rarely, dementia. Also late in the disease, some patients experience severe pain due to muscle cramps, immobility, or pressure sores from being bedridden.

Symptoms and Diagnosis

Persons with the typical symptoms of muscle weakness, muscle cramping, or difficulty speaking or swallowing are generally referred to a neurologist for diagnosis. The neurologist first takes a medical and family history and listens to the patient's and perhaps family members' comments on symptoms. The doctor asks questions about functions such as breathing, speaking, chewing, and swallowing; arm strength; the ability to walk or climb stairs; and so forth. The neurologist also asks about memory loss, vision changes, pain, and the presence of numbness or tingling in an attempt to narrow down the cause of the symptoms and to rule out certain diseases.

Then the physician performs a neurologic examination that evaluates behavior, mood, language, and memory. He or she also inspects the muscles, especially those in the head and neck, for strength, atrophy, and twitching. The muscles in the arms, legs, chest, and abdomen are also evaluated and rated for strength. Usually muscle strength is rated according to the Medical Research Council (MRC) scale ranging from five to zero. A score of five means muscle strength is normal, whereas zero signifies complete paralysis. ALS sufferers in the early stages of the disease typically score a two or a three on muscles affected by the illness. Those in the later phases usually score a one or a zero.

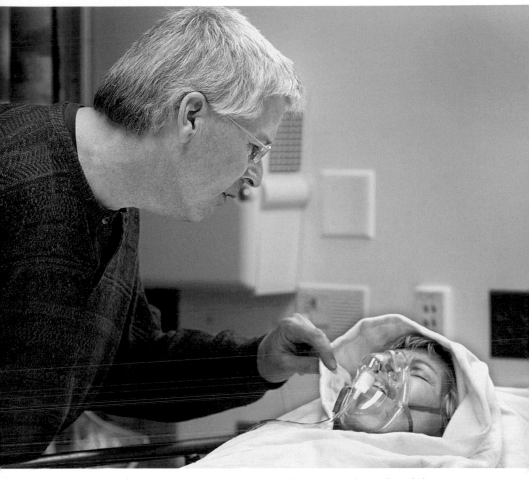

As their disease progresses, patients frequently lose the ability to breathe on their own.

The doctor also assesses muscle tone and reflexes. People with Lou Gehrig's disease typically have abnormal muscle tone and increased reflex activity in which tapping the tendon of one joint leads to reflex activity in adjacent muscles in addition to the expected reflex. The patient is also asked to walk so the doctor can see if his or her gait is abnormal. The physician also performs tests to assess whether the ability to detect a pin-prick on the skin or the feelings of cold or light touch are normal, as these are generally not affected in ALS.

Based on the results of this examination, the doctor arrives at a clinical diagnosis of ALS if there is evidence of muscle

Physicians examine reflexes and muscle tone when diagnosing Lou Gehrig's disease.

weakness, atrophy, and tremors along with abnormal muscle tone, heightened reflexes, and the spread of reflex activity. Then the neurologist orders some laboratory tests to confirm this clinical diagnosis. These laboratory tests include nerve conduction velocity tests, electromyography, neuroimaging of the brain and spinal cord, and blood tests.

Laboratory Tests for Lou Gehrig's Disease

The nerve conduction velocity test calculates how fast individual nerves send electrical impulses to muscles. The speed of this process is generally not affected in ALS, so if it is found to be much reduced, the patient probably does not have the disease. Nerve conduction velocity is measured using patchlike electrodes placed on the skin with tape or a special paste. An electrode that generates a mild electrical shock is placed over the nerve to be analyzed, and an electrode that records muscle contractions is placed over the muscle supplied by that nerve. Brief electrical pulses are sent to the nerve, and the time it takes for the muscle to contract after the electrical pulse arrives is recorded. The speed of the muscle response to the electrical stimulation is called the nerve conduction velocity.

After a nerve conduction velocity test, the doctor performs an electromyography (EMG) test to confirm that motor neurons are not working normally in areas where symptoms are apparent and to detect such abnormalities in areas that do not yet show symptoms. An EMG test involves inserting a needle attached to a recording electrode into a muscle to be tested. The electrode is attached by wires to a recording machine. First, the electrical activity when the muscle is at rest is recorded. Normally there should be no electrical activity recorded when a muscle is at rest, but when ALS is present, the test often shows such activity. Then the doctor performing the test asks the patient to contract the muscle being studied, and the electrical activity generated by this motion is recorded. Contracting the muscle should produce smooth, wavelike forms on the screen of an oscilloscope, or video monitor. But if ALS is present, abnormal waveforms of longer than normal duration appear. Finding these characteristics on an EMG test can help confirm a clinical diagnosis of ALS. After recording from one area of a particular muscle, the physician moves the needle to another area of the muscle or to another muscle to record the electrical activity there. Sometimes a doctor also performs a muscle biopsy, which involves taking a small sample of muscle tissue under local anesthesia and analyzing it in a laboratory for signs of atrophy.

Neuroimaging studies may be done on the brain and spinal cord to check for certain nerve abnormalities sometimes seen in ALS patients. The most common neuroimaging study is an MRI (magnetic resonance imaging). MRI uses a magnetic field and radio waves to create images of the inside of the body. An

EMG Testing

The electromyogram (EMG) test is one of the most important tools in diagnosing amyotrophic lateral sclerosis. The word *electromyogram* means "electrical testing of muscles." The test is performed in a doctor's office, generally by a neurologist, and takes approximately thirty minutes to an hour, depending on how many muscles are tested.

The patient lies on an examination table next to an EMG machine, which looks like a computer. The physician inserts a thin needle into a relaxed muscle and moves the needle inside to record the muscle's activity. Then the patient is asked to move the muscle, and the electrical activity is recorded. The sound of the muscle activity is amplified by the EMG machine and resembles radio static. The electrical activity of the muscle is also displayed on the screen of the EMG machine. The size, duration, and frequency of the electrical signals help determine if there is damage to the muscle or to the nerves leading to the muscle. Usually, the doctor tests five or six muscles in one extremity

MRI machine is a large, cylindrical magnetic tube. When a person is placed inside the tube, radio waves produced by a coil in the machine cause the body to emit faint signals. The machine picks up these signals and processes them through a computer that creates corresponding images from the person's insides. Specially trained doctors can then analyze certain body tissues by the electronic characteristics they display.

Blood tests are also done, mainly to rule out other disorders since the results are generally not abnormal in cases of Lou Gehrig's disease. If blood tests show evidence of a nervous system infection or other abnormality, a doctor may also order a test on the cerebrospinal fluid, the liquid that surrounds the brain and spinal cord. This is known as a spinal tap. It is per-

and then goes on to test in the other extremities. It is fairly painful when the needle is inserted, so some physicians recommend that their patients take pain medication before the test is administered.

The electromyogram (EMG), which tests muscle function, is an important tool in diagnosing Lou Gehrig's disease.

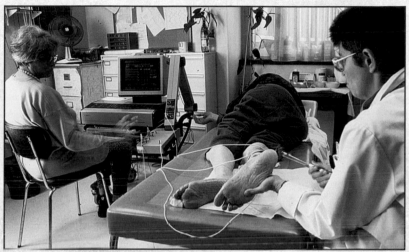

formed by putting a needle into the back between two lower vertebrae and withdrawing the fluid.

Difficulties in Diagnosis

Despite all of these tests, Lou Gehrig's disease is still not an easy condition to diagnose. According to the ALS Association, this is because, "to date, there is no one test or procedure to ultimately establish the diagnosis of ALS. It is through a clinical examination and series of diagnostic tests, often ruling out other diseases that mimic ALS, that a diagnosis can be established."[5]

Some of the diseases that mimic ALS are tumors in the brain stem, multiple small strokes in the brain stem, and multiple sclerosis, an autoimmune disease that produces scarring in the nervous system. An MRI scan can distinguish between

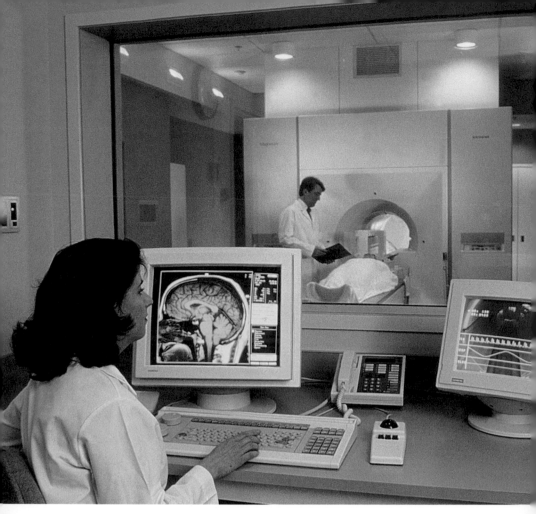

A magnetic resonance imaging (MRI) scan can help doctors distinguish between Lou Gehrig's disease and other disorders that produce similar symptoms.

these diseases and ALS. Several disorders of the spinal cord can also mimic Lou Gehrig's disease. For instance, osteoarthritis of the cervical spine leads to compression of the spinal cord and nerve roots and can cause motor neuron abnormalities in the arms and legs. But this disorder commonly includes pain, which early-stage ALS does not, and disruptions in sensation and bladder and bowel function, which are also not seen in ALS. Various peripheral nerve diseases and some neuromuscular diseases, such as certain forms of muscular dystrophy, can also have symptoms similar to ALS, but the EMG test can differentiate between these disorders.

The Classification of ALS

Once a physician has completed a clinical evaluation and laboratory tests and has diagnosed ALS, he or she classifies the disease based on the degree of diagnostic certainty. This means that the doctor assigns a standardized category to the patient's condition according to how sure he or she is that the patient has ALS. The degree of diagnostic certainty is likely to be less when ALS is in its early stages and symptoms occur only in one body area. When the disease has progressed to involve multiple body regions, it is much easier to arrive at a definite diagnosis.

Neurologists use four categories to describe a diagnosis of ALS. The first category is clinically definite ALS. It is based on clinical evidence that shows both upper and lower motor neuron damage. Upper motor neuron damage is evidenced by exaggerated reflexes and spastic muscles. Lower motor neuron damage is revealed by weak, wasted muscles. In addition, for a diagnosis of clinically definite ALS to be given, at least three of four defined body areas must be affected. The first of these regions is the bulbar region, which includes muscles of the face, mouth, and throat. The cervical area includes muscles of the back of the head, the neck, the shoulders, the upper back, and the arms. The thoracic area includes muscles of the chest, abdomen, and middle portion of the spinal muscles. The lumbosacral area includes muscles of the lower back, groin, and legs.

The second diagnostic category, clinically probable ALS, involves clinical evidence of upper and lower motor neuron damage in at least two body regions, with some upper motor neuron damage signs located above the lower motor neuron signs. This means that the symptoms of upper motor neuron damage must be present in areas of the body that are located physically above those areas that show symptoms of lower motor neuron damage. For example, if a patient has exaggerated reflexes and spastic muscles in one hand and weakness and wasted muscles in one leg, a diagnosis of clinically probable ALS can be made. The location of the symptoms is important

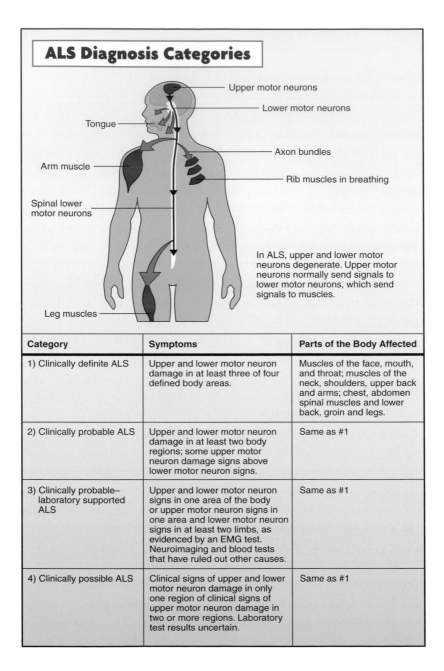

ALS Diagnosis Categories

Upper motor neurons
Lower motor neurons
Tongue
Axon bundles
Arm muscle
Rib muscles in breathing
Spinal lower
motor neurons
Leg muscles

In ALS, upper and lower motor neurons degenerate. Upper motor neurons normally send signals to lower motor neurons, which send signals to muscles.

Category	Symptoms	Parts of the Body Affected
1) Clinically definite ALS	Upper and lower motor neuron damage in at least three of four defined body areas.	Muscles of the face, mouth, and throat; muscles of the neck, shoulders, upper back and arms; chest, abdomen spinal muscles and lower back, groin and legs.
2) Clinically probable ALS	Upper and lower motor neuron damage in at least two body regions; some upper motor neuron damage signs above lower motor neuron signs.	Same as #1
3) Clinically probable–laboratory supported ALS	Upper and lower motor neuron signs in one area of the body or upper motor neuron signs in one area and lower motor neuron signs in at least two limbs, as evidenced by an EMG test. Neuroimaging and blood tests that have ruled out other causes.	Same as #1
4) Clinically possible ALS	Clinical signs of upper and lower motor neuron damage in only one region of clinical signs of upper motor neuron damage in two or more regions. Laboratory test results uncertain.	Same as #1

because neurologists use this data to determine the extent of upper and lower motor neuron involvement.

The third diagnostic category is clinically probable–laboratory supported ALS. This is assigned to a patient who shows clinical signs of upper and lower motor neuron damage in one area.

Clinically probable–laboratory supported ALS can also apply to someone who has upper motor neuron signs in one area and lower motor neuron signs present in at least two limbs, as evidenced by an EMG test. In addition to the EMG test, this category requires that the physician perform certain neuroimaging and blood tests to rule out other causes for the patient's symptoms.

The fourth diagnostic category is clinically possible ALS. This is assigned to a patient who shows clinical signs of upper and lower motor neuron damage in only one body region. It can also be assigned to someone who shows upper motor neuron signs alone in two or more regions. Lastly, clinically probable ALS applies to a patient who shows lower motor neuron signs above upper motor neuron signs. This means that the person shows weak, wasted muscles in a body region above a region where upper motor neuron damage is apparent. Laboratory test results also must be uncertain, and other diagnoses must have been excluded for this category to apply.

Besides labeling a diagnosis of ALS with one of these four categories, doctors also distinguish the diagnosis on the basis of how the disease is acquired. There are two ways that Lou Gehrig's disease can be acquired: sporadic and familial. Ninety to 95 percent of cases of ALS are sporadic, meaning their origin is unknown. The other 5 to 10 percent of Lou Gehrig's disease patients have an inherited form of the disease called familial ALS. This form is identified by means of a family history. A neurologist or a genetic counselor asks whether anyone else in the family has been diagnosed with ALS or has had progressive muscular weakness and breathing problems. If so, this is a good indication of the familial form of the disease.

After the Diagnosis

Once ALS has been diagnosed, it is difficult for a doctor to predict how fast the disease will progress, as this varies greatly from patient to patient. Whereas some patients die within a few months after the onset of symptoms, others have lived for more than thirty years. The longest documented durations of ALS have been thirty-two and thirty-nine years. The average length of time between the onset of symptoms and death, however, is two to four years. Experts say this makes ALS one of the most serious and destructive illnesses:

> ALS is one of the most devastating diseases of humankind. It results in death within months or years from diagnosis, following a progressive, complete paralysis of extremities, respiratory muscles, and bulbar (relating to speech and swallowing) muscles, with the affected person remaining cognitively intact and thus aware of the incapacitating symptoms.[6]

Age is one factor that influences how long an ALS sufferer lives. The younger the patient, the longer he or she generally survives. By contrast, those with worse symptoms at diagnosis and those with a short interval between symptom onset and diagnosis tend to live for a shorter time. One study showed that patients with stronger psychological health lived longer. Other research has shown that patients whose early symptoms involve the arms and legs live longer than those whose early symptoms involve speech, swallowing, and respiratory symptoms. In very few patients, the progression of ALS suddenly stops with no apparent reason, increasing survival time. Even though these research studies offer some predictions on who is likely to survive for a longer or shorter time, each patient is different, and his or her symptoms may progress in an unpredictable manner. Thus, after a diagnosis of ALS is made, the physician and patient must adopt a wait-and-see attitude.

CHAPTER TWO

What Causes Lou Gehrig's Disease?

Lou Gehrig's disease is caused by the destruction of certain cells in the central nervous system. The central nervous system is made up of neurons and glial cells in the brain and spinal cord. Neurons transmit information using electrical impulses and chemical messengers known as neurotransmitters. Glial cells support neurons.

Neurons have three major parts. One is the cell body, which contains a nucleus that controls the cell's activities and houses the DNA, or genetic information. The other parts are axons and dendrites. Axons look like long tails. They transmit messages from the cell. Dendrites look like tree branches. They receive messages for the cell. Neurons communicate through these axons and dendrites by sending neurotransmitters across tiny spaces known as synapses. These neurotransmitters can either excite or calm a neuron. If the neuron is excited, it generates an electrical impulse that triggers the release of a neurotransmitter to send to the next neuron, and so on.

There are three major classes of neurons. Sensory neurons carry information from the sense organs, such as the eyes and ears, to the brain. Motor neurons have long axons and carry information from the central nervous system to muscles throughout the body. Interneurons are the third major class of neurons. They communicate only in their individual area through short axons.

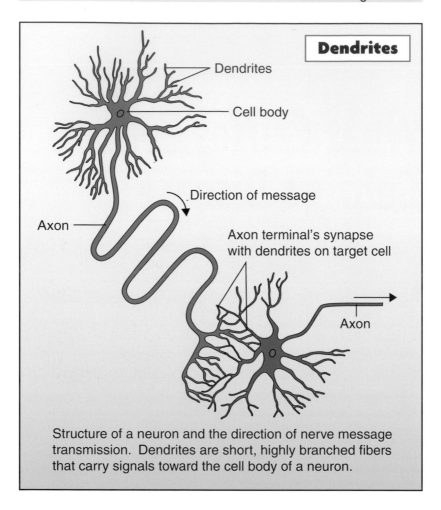

Dendrites

Dendrites

Cell body

Direction of message

Axon

Axon terminal's synapse
with dendrites on target cell

Axon

Structure of a neuron and the direction of nerve message
transmission. Dendrites are short, highly branched fibers
that carry signals toward the cell body of a neuron.

The Types of Motor Neurons

ALS affects the motor neurons in the brain and spinal cord. The
two subtypes of motor neurons, upper motor neurons and lower
motor neurons, are both affected. Upper motor neurons are so
named because they are found mainly in a region of the upper
brain called the motor cortex. Some upper motor neurons are
found in the brain stem. The axons of upper motor neurons connect with and send messages to lower motor neurons, which are
located in the brain stem and spinal cord. Lower motor neurons
got their name because they are located lower down in the body
than are upper motor neurons. The long axons of lower motor

neurons, in turn, connect with and send messages to muscles throughout the body.

Although ALS affects motor neurons, patients may not notice any muscle weakness or other symptoms during the earliest stage of the disease. This is because axons belonging to healthy motor neurons develop sprouts and take control of muscle fibers that are connected to the diseased neurons. But as the illness progresses, the rate of degeneration of motor neurons exceeds the rate of new connections, and symptoms become apparent.

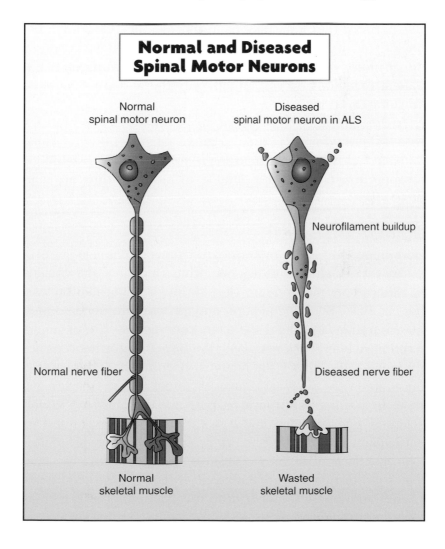

Normal and Diseased Spinal Motor Neurons

Normal spinal motor neuron

Diseased spinal motor neuron in ALS

Neurofilament buildup

Normal nerve fiber

Diseased nerve fiber

Normal skeletal muscle

Wasted skeletal muscle

Damage to upper motor neurons and lower motor neurons produces different symptoms. Since the primary function of upper motor neurons is to control voluntary movements, reflexes, and muscle tone, when these neurons are damaged in ALS, reflexes become exaggerated and limbs become spastic. The destruction of upper motor neurons in the top part of the brain may also lead to the emotional outbursts that occur in some ALS patients. Without the control normally exerted by these upper motor neurons, which activate muscles in the face and throat involved in laughing and crying, more primitive parts of the brain take over and produce emotional behavior that would normally be inhibited. The destruction of upper motor neurons does not influence the emotions that a patient feels, however. It affects only the actual behavior of laughing or crying.

Lower motor neurons primarily send signals to muscles to tell them when it is time to move or stop moving. Thus, damage to lower motor neurons results in weak, wasted, or atrophic muscles that are unable to move as they are supposed to.

Similar Diseases

Both upper and lower motor neuron signs of damage are necessary for a diagnosis of ALS. Sometimes a patient shows signs of either upper motor neuron loss or lower motor neuron loss, but not both. Such a condition may progress to become ALS, but sometimes it is the result of another disease. For example, in primary lateral sclerosis only the upper motor neurons are damaged. This causes the limbs to become stiff and spastic, but there is not the muscle atrophy found in Lou Gehrig's disease. In some cases, however, patients with primary lateral sclerosis later develop lower motor neuron damage and its subsequent symptoms. Doctors refer to this as upper motor neuron–onset ALS. In progressive muscular atrophy, only lower motor neurons are damaged. If this disease progresses to ALS with upper motor neuron involvement, it is known as lower motor neuron–onset ALS.

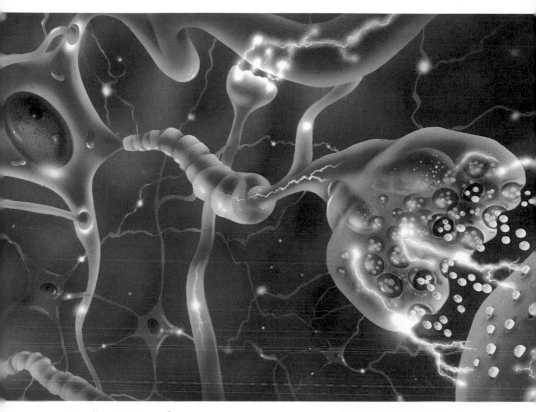

An illustration of an upper motor neuron sending a nerve impulse. Damage to neurons caused by ALS causes reflexes to become exaggerated and limbs to become spastic.

Underlying Causes

While experts are certain that the destruction of upper and lower motor neurons causes symptoms of ALS, the underlying cause of this neuron destruction probably involves multiple factors. According to the Muscular Dystrophy Association, "Years ago, it was widely believed that there might be one cause to explain all cases of ALS. Today, doctors and scientists know that can't be the case. Together, they're working to identify the multiple causes of this disorder."

Among the suggested underlying causes for ALS over the years have been dietary deficiencies, infections, vascular disorders (disorders of the blood vessels), exposure to environmental

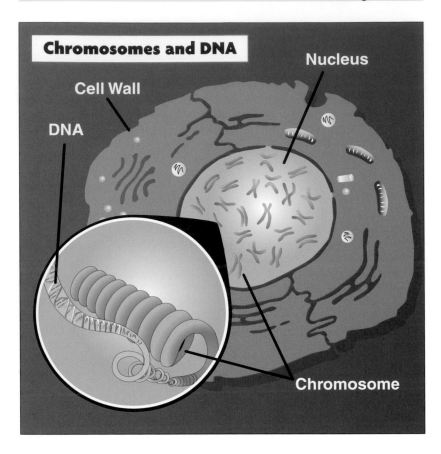

Chromosomes and DNA

Nucleus

Cell Wall

DNA

Chromosome

toxins, and antibodies to neurons or other body tissues. Also studied as possible causes have been disorders of neuron function, genetic disorders, physical injury, growth factors, premature aging, and imbalances of certain neurotransmitters. One factor that has been proven to play a role in one type of ALS, the familial variety, is genetic mutations.

Genes and ALS

Genes are made up of deoxyribonucleic acid (DNA) and transmit hereditary information from parents to their offspring. They reside on wormlike bodies called chromosomes in the center, or nucleus, of each cell. The sequence of genes on each chromosome provides the cell containing those chromosomes with a set of instructions on how to grow and operate.

A baby is born with two copies of this instruction set—one from each parent.

Humans have forty-six chromosomes in each cell, with the exception of mature sex cells, which determine the sex of the offspring and which have only twenty-three chromosomes. Twenty-three of the forty-six chromosomes in most cells come from the mother, and the other twenty-three come from the father. The genes on each chromosome also come in pairs, with one copy of every gene from the mother and one from the father.

When a gene or chromosome is damaged, the resulting change is called a mutation. Mutated genetic material can be passed to a child if it happens to be part of the set of chromosomes and genes transmitted from either the mother or the father. When this occurs, the altered genetic instructions may cause various malfunctions that produce certain diseases or disorders.

The most common inheritance pattern for the mutated genes that cause familial ALS is called autosomal dominant. *Autosomal* means that it is equally likely that a male or female will inherit a gene mutation. *Dominant* means that a person needs only one mutated gene in a gene pair, randomly passed on from either the mother or the father, to have an increased risk of getting familial ALS. Some diseases or traits are determined by a recessive gene rather than a dominant one. When a gene is recessive, both genes in a pair must be mutated in order for the disease or trait to be transmitted.

Gene Mutations Linked to ALS

In 1993 Dr. Daniel R. Rosen and his colleagues at Massachusetts General Hospital first discovered a dominant gene mutation present in 15 to 20 percent of cases of familial ALS. Members of families in which this gene mutation occurs have a 50 percent chance of inheriting it and developing the disease. Using sophisticated DNA sequencing and identification techniques, these researchers proved that this particular gene mutation causes Lou Gehrig's disease. The mutation is in the superoxide dismutase (SOD1) gene. SOD1 is involved with balancing free radicals in cells. Free radicals are very unstable molecules produced in the body that interact quickly with other chemicals. When free radicals are not neutralized by the body, cell damage can result. Researchers believe that the SOD1 gene mutation affects an enzyme that normally limits the production of free radicals. The mutated gene produces an enzyme that cannot do this, and the resulting free radical activity damages motor neurons and leads to symptoms of ALS.

Researchers have linked mutations besides the SOD1 gene mutation to familial ALS, but they have not yet proven that these mutations actually cause the disease. In 2003 several teams of researchers found four families with an as-yet-unidentified gene mutation on chromosome sixteen. This opens up the possibility of identifying another gene mutation that causes familial ALS. Explains Dr. Lucie Bruijn, science director and vice president of the ALS Association, "The next step—identification of the mutant gene—will have enormous impact on ALS research, similar to that of the SOD1 discovery in 1993."[8] Because the researchers have already isolated the location of the mutant gene to one particular area on chromosome sixteen, they are hopeful the gene can be identified quickly.

Also in 2003, research by a group of European investigators has pointed to the VEGF gene as another gene that may contribute to the development of ALS. *VEGF* stands for "vascular endothelial growth factor." A growth factor is a chemical that aids the growth of cells. The VEGF gene produces a growth factor that aids in the development of the vascular (blood vessel) system. The researchers found that mice with low VEGF levels showed motor neuron degeneration and became paralyzed. This suggests that VEGF might have an important influence on motor neurons. Further studies have been undertaken to see if giving VEGF to animals with ALS will improve their condition. Investigators are also trying to figure out if the low levels of VEGF result from a VEGF gene mutation or from other genetic factors combined with this mutation. The scien-

How Is a Genetic Test for ALS Done?

Persons who have a family history of ALS can have a genetic test done to see if they have the SOD1 gene mutation responsible for the familial form of the disease. A genetic counselor writing for the ALS Association explains how such a test is performed:

A blood sample is taken and sent to a specialized lab where the genetic material, also called DNA, is removed. Special laboratory techniques allow the SOD1 gene to be replicated and then tested. One form of testing is running the sample on a gel to generate a series of bands. If a genetic change is present, the bands will be in a different location compared to a control sample, which is known not to have a genetic change in the SOD1 gene. . . . Another method called sequencing may also be used to either initially test or confirm results. Sequencing is able to view the DNA on a finer scale by displaying the actual letters of the "instruction book" [chemicals that make up the genetic code] so that changes can be seen.

This test usually takes two to three months to complete. A positive result confirms that an individual has the SOD1 mutation responsible for some forms of familial ALS. But a negative result does not mean that the person does not carry a gene for familial ALS; it only means that the SOD1 gene mutation is not present. There are other forms of familial ALS whose genes have not yet been identified.

tists have discovered that humans with any one of three variations in the VEGF gene had a 1.8 times greater risk than the general population of developing Lou Gehrig's disease. These three variations all led to lower than normal blood levels of VEGF in these people; thus, it is likely that low levels of VEGF are related to the development of ALS, but the exact manner in which this works is not yet clear.

This illustration depicts molecules called free radicals attacking cells and tissues. Damage to motor neurons by free radicals leads to symptoms of ALS.

Other Possible Causes

Besides evidence for genetic mutations that can cause ALS, scientists have also discovered several other biochemical factors that may help cause the disease. One factor is an excess of the neurotransmitter glutamate in the brain and spinal cord of patients with ALS. When there is too much glutamate around motor neurons, it appears that these neurons are damaged and can then die. The excess glutamate seems to occur because of several factors: First, the nervous system produces and releases excess amounts of glutamate; second, there may be defects in glutamate receptors on receiving neurons' dendrites; and third, a protein known as EAAT2 is deficient. Since EAAT2 is responsible for clearing glutamate from the synapses between neurons, a deficiency thus results in an excess of glutamate. The cause of the EAAT2 deficiency may be a genetic mutation or other factor, but scientists do not know for sure.

Another research finding that may shed light on the causes of ALS involves antibodies—that is, chemicals produced by the immune system in response to an antigen, or foreign substance, such as a virus or bacterium. Sometimes the body produces antibodies to its own cells; this is known as an autoimmune reaction. Many ALS patients have antibodies to calcium channels, which are membrane openings that regulate the flow of calcium into neurons. The antibodies prevent the channels from working properly, leading to a sustained influx of calcium into the neurons that may result in cell damage or death.

Some scientists have suggested that proteins known as neurofilaments play a role in causing ALS. Neurofilaments are chemicals that help neurons maintain their shape. In neurons affected by Lou Gehrig's disease, these neurofilaments clump together near the body of the cell. When they do this, they are not able to move down the cell's axon, as would happen in a normal cell. However, the relationship between neurofilament clumping, the loss of ability to move down the axon, and ALS has not yet been established.

Damage to DNA in the mitochondria, or powerhouse, of nerve cells is another process that may play a role in the development of ALS, though this has not been proven. It appears that there is more mitochondrial damage in ALS-affected cells than in normal cells, which usually sustain some such damage as a result of aging. Whether the increased mitochondrial damage results from or causes ALS remains to be seen.

What Triggers the Cellular Damage in ALS?

Whether it is excess glutamate, excess calcium, or damage to neurofilaments or mitochondria that leads to motor neuron degeneration, the question remains as to what factors trigger these cellular conditions and the resulting damage. Over the years a great many possibilities have been suggested. One theory is that a virus is the culprit. In 1875 Jean-Martin Charcot wondered if a link existed between the polio virus and the subsequent development of ALS since the polio virus causes paralysis. But there has been no conclusive evidence linking polio or any other virus to Lou Gehrig's disease. Still, however, researchers continue to study this issue.

One study found traces of a type of virus called an echovirus in ALS patients' spinal cord tissue, but this study has not been replicated. Other scientists have looked at prions, which are proteins that act like viruses but can be even more deadly. Prions change normal tissue into toxic molecules and often act on the nervous system, so they are being analyzed for a possible role in ALS. Still other researchers have studied the possibility that retroviruses contribute to ALS. A retrovirus is a virus that stores its genetic information as RNA (ribonucleic acid) rather than as DNA. Investigators recently found that a significant proportion of ALS patients have a chemical associated with retroviruses in their blood. Said one of the researchers, Jeremy A. Gerson of University College London, "This is a very exciting finding that points towards the possibility of retrovirus involvement in ALS. However, much work remains to be done and we are very much aware that in virology, as in other branches of medical science, finding an association is not the same as proving a cause."[9]

Another factor that has been suggested as an underlying cause of Lou Gehrig's disease in some patients is smoking. Doctors at Baystate Medical Center in Springfield, Massachusetts, found that smoking cigarettes makes people more likely to develop sporadic ALS. Whether smoking actually causes the disease—and, if so, how this occurs—is not yet known, however.

The Aids Virus and ALS

Although most research has found no link between viruses and Lou Gehrig's disease, several doctors have reported on a form of ALS in AIDS patients that improves or disappears with treatment for AIDS. This form of ALS may not be identical to the usual form of the disease that gets progressively worse, but understanding its characteristics could lead to breakthroughs in treating the usual type.

Following treatment for AIDS, several patients in France and in New York who had also been diagnosed with ALS recovered from the ALS. These patients were treated with protease inhibitors, drugs that work partly by preventing certain white blood cells from dying. Doctors hypothesized that protease inhibitors also may prevent motor neurons from dying; thus, the inhibitors had an effect on the patients' ALS. However, when people with ALS but not AIDS were given a protease inhibitor in a clinical trial, no improvement in the ALS occurred. Therefore, it appears that cases of reversible ALS in AIDS patients have different causes than cases of traditional ALS. Experts theorize that the ALS-like syndrome that occurs in some AIDS patients may be a result of these patients' weakened immune systems, which render their bodies unable to suppress nerve damage to motor neurons. When the immune system is made stronger by protease inhibitors, the neurons apparently recover.

Experts have long suspected that exposure to toxins like gasoline, lead, and heavy metals may cause ALS, but again there is no proof that this is true. Some researchers have found that people with ALS have had higher exposure to lead and heavy metals compared to control groups, and others have found high levels of aluminum and manganese in the soil and drinking water in regions of the western Pacific, where the incidence of ALS was fifty to one hundred times higher than normal at the beginning of the twentieth century. But other research has shown that exposure to lead and heavy metals causes reversible ALS-like symptoms that are not true instances of the disease, so the question is still open.

Some scientists have also suggested that something in the diet of the inhabitants of the western Pacific Islands with high rates of ALS may have contributed to the disease. In Guam, for example, researchers linked an elevated incidence of ALS in the native Chamorro people to eating flying fox bats, which contain significant levels of the neurotoxin b-methylamino-L-alanine (BMAA). Chamorro people who died from ALS had

American veterans of the 1991 Persian Gulf War have a much higher incidence of Lou Gehrig's disease than the general population.

high levels of BMAA in their brains, while healthy brain tissue does not contain this chemical. Still, no one has actually proven that BMAA causes ALS.

Further evidence that something in the diet or in the environment may contribute to ALS comes from other so-called clusters of the disease. Cases in which both partners in a married couple develop ALS have been reported in the United States, Italy, and France. There have also been small regional clusters of the disease, in which several people were diagnosed around the same time, reported in Two Rivers, Wisconsin; Montreal, Canada; Burlington, North Carolina; and rural South Dakota. No one, however, has been able to pinpoint a specific environmental toxin or even a common infection that could explain these cases.

Health authorities are now studying a population of U.S. veterans who were deployed to the Persian Gulf in the 1991 Gulf War to try to determine why this group of people have twice the incidence of ALS as other veterans. Researchers are interviewing those affected to find out where they served and to which environmental toxins they may have been exposed. Comments Mary Lyon, vice president of patient services for the ALS Association, "The Gulf War ALS study should serve as a source of incremental knowledge in a body of future research to learn more about the occurrence of ALS in military veterans. This information, in turn, can lead to a better understanding of ALS and how one or more environmental exposures may contribute to the disease."[10]

Another question that remains unanswered is why military veterans in general, not just from the Gulf War, have higher than normal rates of ALS. A report released by the ALS Association in May 2005 reveals that both male and female veterans have a nearly 60 percent greater risk of ALS than nonveterans. "If you serve in the military, regardless of the branch of service, regardless of whether you served in the Persian Gulf War, Vietnam, Korea, or World War II, and regardless of whether you served during a time of peace or a time of war, you are at greater risk of dying from ALS than if you had not served in the military,"[11] said Steve Gibson, vice president for government relations and public affairs of the ALS Association.

An Unresolved Question

Although it would simplify matters if researchers could uncover a single cause for Lou Gehrig's disease, it is not likely that this will occur. Rather, it appears that a variety of environmental and cellular factors may contribute to the nerve damage that characterizes ALS. Pinpointing what these factors are will potentially lead to effective treatments for the disease.

How Is Lou Gehrig's Disease Treated?

Treatment for Lou Gehrig's disease may be received in a variety of health care settings. Some patients go to comprehensive ALS clinics that coordinate care among various specialists. For example, the Cleveland Clinic offers a weekly ALS program in which a neurologist, a nurse coordinator, and a physical therapist see the patient. The team also includes an occupational therapist, a speech pathologist, a dietician, and a social worker. Other specialists such as lung doctors or home health care providers are called in as needed.

Helping the patient to remain independent and perform as many normal activities as possible for as long as possible is the goal of the ALS treatment team. Each member tries to help the patient maintain mobility, continue to feed and dress himself or herself, communicate, and pursue hobbies or work.

Experts find that a coordinated treatment team gives ALS patients the best care because their needs are constantly changing and can be immediately addressed. When such a specialized clinic is not available, experts recommend that the patient see a neurologist who has experience treating ALS. The neurologist then makes referrals to other specialists as needed.

The neurologist is primarily responsible for treating Lou Gehrig's disease. This doctor prescribes and orders complementary treatments and medications needed to relieve symptoms and monitors the patient's progress and response to therapy. The neurologist also provides the patient with information on the disease and on treatments that are likely to be needed later on, such as a feeding tube or a mechanical ventilator. Neurologists also may advise the patient on how to enter research studies on new treatments for the disease.

ALS patients are treated primarily by neurologists, doctors who specialize in the nervous system.

A neurologist's management of Lou Gehrig's disease is aided by the ALS Patient Care Database, a service that records data on treatment and care submitted by neurologists and patients. The information submitted is kept confidential by coding the names of participants. It is sent to doctors who specialize in treating ALS to give them data on what measures work best during various stages of the disease.

Drug Treatment

One critical aspect of treatment for ALS patients is medications used to prolong life and to ease various symptoms. Many drugs and nutritional supplements have been tried for treatment of the disease, with one of the most common being Vitamin E. In fact, Lou Gehrig received daily injections of Vitamin E to treat his ALS. However, researchers have not been able to show that Vitamin E provides any benefit to humans with Lou Gehrig's disease. Many neurologists continue to recommend its use, though, since it has been found to slow the progression of ALS in mice.

Currently, only one medication is approved by the U.S. Food and Drug Administration (FDA) for treatment of ALS. That drug is riluzole, brand name Rilutek, which has been shown to prolong survival in patients by two to three months and slightly delay the need for breathing support. Patients on riluzole show no improvement and indeed may not be able to tell that the medication is slowing the course of the disease because they do not know how fast the disease would have progressed without the drug. Still, however, the FDA has determined that riluzole does slow the progression of the disease slightly and it is therefore prescribed for many ALS patients.

Besides riluzole, doctors also prescribe other drugs to people with ALS to relieve specific symptoms, such as muscle cramps and spasms, excessive crying or laughing, depression, and shortness of breath. When oral medications do not adequately treat certain symptoms, sometimes doctors implant a pump in the spinal cord to administer medication directly through the nervous system.

Other Treatments for Disability

Drug treatments for ALS are only a small part of the therapy required for the patient to maintain independence and a good quality of life for as long as possible. Other types of therapy require the services of several different specialists who are often consulted to assist the person with varying and changing needs. One such specialist is an occupational therapist, who offers advice on and helps the patient obtain tools that compensate for muscle weakness when performing daily activities like feeding, dressing, and bathing. An occupational therapist can recommend devices like button and zipper hooks, doorknob extenders, long-handled cups, grab bars, raised toilet seats, ramps, and shower benches. He or she can help people find items like lift cushions, which are special cushions that

Occupational therapists can help the ALS patient to obtain tools that compensate for muscle weakness when performing daily activities.

More About Riluzole

Riluzole is currently the only drug approved specifically for the treatment of ALS. Experts believe that it protects motor neurons from damage caused by too much of the neurotransmitter gluta- mate. While riluzole cannot restore muscle function that is already lost, studies show that it does keep patients alive longer than con- trol groups of patients given a placebo, or sugar pill. More than eleven hundred people participated in clinical trials for riluzole. During the first year of treatment, patients who took riluzole had a much better chance of staying alive than did patients given the placebo. But after eighteen months, both groups had an equal chance of dying from ALS. This indicates that the protective ef- fects of riluzole do not last longer than a year for most patients.

Common side effects of riluzole are weakness, nausea, lung- function decrease, headache, dizziness, and fatigue. Sometimes riluzole can cause liver or kidney problems, so doctors recom- mend that people on the drug get frequent blood tests to check liver and kidney function.

Although riluzole has only a modest effect on prolonging survival in ALS patients, it is the first drug that has achieved any effect at all on the progression of the disease. Experts and pa- tients alike hope that the biochemical characteristics of this drug can be further developed to lead to drugs that have a more profound effect on the course of the disease.

make it easier to rise from a seated position. A lift cushion may be adequate for a time, but a mechanical lift may be required as weakness progresses. Similarly, a walker may suffice for help with walking at first, but soon the patient may need a wheelchair to get around and a chair lift to get up and down stairs.

The decision to get a wheelchair is usually a difficult and traumatic one for patients and families, in large part because a wheelchair is a symbol of disability and it is not easy to admit that an individual is incapacitated to the point of needing one. Experts say, however, that once a patient has started to give up activities because of a lack of mobility, and once walking takes up most of the person's strength and energy, it is usually time to get a wheelchair. Either an occupational therapist or a physical therapist can provide guidance in choosing the right wheelchair.

Closely related to the assistance provided by an occupational therapist is that provided by a physical therapist. A phys-

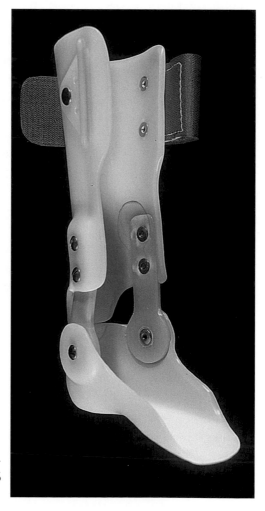

Braces such as this ankle-leg orthosis can help ALS patients remain mobile.

ical therapist assesses physical functions and teaches the patient various exercises so as to maintain limb function and mobility as long as possible. He or she evaluates the motion of joints, muscle strength, and endurance, and may employ massage techniques or apply heat or cold to treat pain or cramps. Physical therapists can also provide devices like ankle/foot orthoses to compensate for foot drop and knee sleeves to compensate for buckling of the legs. Orthoses are limb braces that help stabilize and support a joint. An ankle/foot orthosis supports and strengthens weakened feet and ankles. It is made of metal, plastic, or a combination of these materials. A knee sleeve is made of heavy fabric that fits over and supports the knee. Sometimes a physical therapist sends a patient to an orthotist, or specialist in orthopedic appliances, who designs and builds appliances that support or properly align joints that become deformed by ALS. Examples are special neck braces to support weakened neck muscles and ankle braces to support weakened ankles.

In the early stages of ALS, physical therapists usually recommend that patients do stretching, strength training, and aerobic exercise. As muscle weakness develops, muscles that are not used quickly lose the ability to move, so stretching them is important. Strength training is done with weights. Examples of aerobic exercise, which raises the heart rate, are walking, swimming, or running. Experts recommend that patients do as much exercise as they are able to without falling or getting too fatigued. "Don't push yourself too hard, avoid exercises that pose an obvious risk of injury, and work closely with a rehabilitation specialist or physical therapist who can recommend adjustments to your program as your abilities change,"[12] says Dan Stimson of the Muscular Dystrophy Association.

Therapy for Eating and Communication Difficulties

As a patient's mouth and throat muscles weaken, chewing and swallowing may become increasingly difficult. A speech therapist may be consulted to evaluate the person's level of dysfunction and to recommend foods that are more easily consumed. The speech therapist often works in conjunction with a professional dietitian who assesses how well nourished the patient is and makes recommendations to ensure adequate nutrition and prevent weight loss. For example, the dietitian may design a meal plan and may counsel a patient who becomes fatigued from eating to eat smaller, more frequent meals rather than larger ones.

Once an ALS patient can no longer swallow food, a feeding tube may have to be surgically placed into the stomach by a gastroenterologist, or specialist in the digestive system. This is called a percutaneous gastronomy (PEG) tube. A PEG tube may also be needed when the patient can still swallow but tends to take food or drink into the lungs, creating a danger of pneumonia. In some cases, a patient can continue to consume small amounts of food or drink by mouth even after a PEG tube is inserted. This helps preserve the person's quality of life for as long as possible.

A speech therapist is also consulted for assistance with speech difficulties. At first an ALS sufferer's speech may become imprecise, slurred, nasal, soft, or breathless. Later on, speech may become impossible. A speech therapist can recommend several things at each stage of functioning. As explained by the Muscular Dystrophy Association:

> Early in the disease process, while speech is still normal or nearly so, speech therapists may suggest that a person with ALS record his or her speech. A number of phrases can later be programmed into a computer, or perhaps the person would like to talk about his or her life for future listening by friends and family. Later, the therapist can teach the person with ALS special techniques for conserving energy and making speech understood as well as possible. In some cases, a dentist can be asked to make a device called a palatal lift that can help compensate for certain types of muscle weakness. Later still, the therapist can help the person with ALS learn to use an electronic device that can substitute for speech.[13]

Weakened throat and mouth muscles can make speech difficult for ALS patients. Speech therapists can help patients regain their ability to communicate.

In the first stages of the disease, some patients also benefit from a microphone to make speech louder. As speech weakens, many use an alphabet board or erasable board to communicate. Those who cannot write or point at letters can use an Eye-Link, which has the alphabet organized on a sheet of clear plastic. The ALS patient looks directly at each letter of the word he or she wishes to communicate, and the eye gaze serves as the "pointer" for each letter. There are also electronic systems that track sustained eye gazes for

Physicist Stephen Hawking uses a computerized speech synthesizer to communicate.

communication. For talking on the telephone, some ALS patients rely on a telecommunications device for the deaf, which they can use to type in a message rather than speak. The person on the other end of the line can speak normally into the phone.

Some patients use a regular computer to communicate when they can no longer speak. If they are unable to use a standard mouse, there are alternatives such as a trackball or a head mouse. A trackball can be rolled in a variety of directions using small motions of the fingers. A head mouse consists of a small sensor strapped to the forehead that directs a beam of light to the computer screen and is controlled by small movements of the head.

For communication away from home, dedicated communication systems are available. Dedicated communication systems run on batteries and include a keyboard for typing in messages. Some include a synthetic voice output or printed output in response to what is typed in. Some are activated by scanning with the eyes rather than with a keyboard.

In the late stages of ALS, muscle weakness may be so profound that the patient can only blink his or her eyes or breathe to control a computer or voice synthesizer. In this case, a switch that bypasses a computer keyboard can be activated by blinking the eyes or breathing in a predetermined code pattern such as Morse code. This switch can be hooked up to an electronic communication device that translates the eye blinks or breaths into letters.

Other Treatment Specialists

Besides the speech therapist, another member of the multidisciplinary ALS care team is a social worker. This specialist assesses the emotional status of the patient and assists with the patient's home care needs and living arrangements. This includes determining whether a family member is capable of caring for the patient full time at home and making arrangements for hospitalization or hospice care for acute problems or end-of-life care. The social worker can also help with financial issues or concerns and can make referrals for psychiatric or psychological care.

Many patients become depressed or anxious about their condition and require a mental health professional to help deal with these problems. A psychiatrist is a medical doctor who can prescribe medications to treat depression or anxiety. Psychologists are doctors who treat mental disorders through talking and behavioral therapy. They strive to get the patient to talk about any problems and to cope by changing behaviors and thoughts.

Another specialist that becomes part of an ALS treatment team is a pulmonologist, or breathing specialist. Early on in the disease, a physical therapist can show the patient how to cough and breathe more easily by leaning forward or by positioning the head in a particular way. But later on, a pulmonary specialist is generally needed to prescribe one of several types of ventilators to assist the person with breathing. Some patients do well with a noninvasive ventilator, which has a fan that pushes air through a mask or through short plastic tubes placed into the nostrils. Most ALS patients use this kind of device. This supports the mechanical task of breathing and gives the weakened breathing muscles a break from working. Later on, many patients need invasive ventilation. Here, a surgical opening is

Most ALS patients eventually need to use a ventilator to help them breathe.

made in the airway and is hooked up to a mechanical ventilator.

Choosing whether to obtain invasive mechanical ventilation is one of the most difficult decisions a patient and family must make. This is often because of financial considerations or because of an unwillingness to live by artificial life support. The twenty-four-hour-a-day care that a person on ventilator support requires is very expensive, especially if this care is administered in a hospital or a nursing home. If family members elect to perform this continuous care at home, it requires a round-the-clock time commitment, as the patient is no longer able to care for him- or herself. Many patients who view an existence hooked up to a ventilator as lacking in any quality of life elect not to undergo this form of treatment and instead opt to be made as comfortable as possible until death occurs.

The Timing of Assistive Devices

Different patients incorporate different treatment specialists and assistive devices into their care regimen at different stages of their disease, but experts agree that it is a good idea to confront these issues before they are really needed and to plan ahead for increasing disability. As Will, an ALS patient, advises other patients:

> Stay ahead of the curve. Get a wheelchair when walking difficulties begin, even though you can still walk. Get a feeding tube before you lose weight. Begin using augmentative communication aids before you need them. Get respiratory support by using a BiPAP [a noninvasive ventilator] at night as soon as possible. By taking these and other steps early, you remain in control. No one with the disease regrets doing these things early; many regret waiting too long.[14]

Alternative Therapies

Besides the conventional medical treatments of drugs and assistive devices for Lou Gehrig's disease, many patients also seek alternative therapies. However, none of these alternative

The Recommended Diet for ALS Patients

Doctors and dietitians recommend that ALS patients eat a well-balanced diet that gives them adequate amounts of calories, protein, vitamins, and minerals. This helps maintain muscles and fat as much as possible despite the progression of the disease. According to experts at the ALS Association, a balanced diet should include servings from each of four food groups each day. A patient, they say, should consume three or more servings from the meat and protein group, two or more servings per day of milk, four or more servings of fruits and vegetables, and four or more servings of grains. Doctors say that people with ALS should not skimp on portions or try to lose weight, even if they are overweight, because as the disease progresses, consuming adequate nutrition will become more and more difficult.

therapies is known to slow the progression of the disease, though some may improve the quality of the person's life somewhat. Doctors caution that before trying any such therapy patients should check with their physician to ensure that the therapy cannot do them harm.

Antioxidants are one common type of complementary treatment. These supplements remove dangerous cell-damaging free radicals from the body. Vitamins E, C, and beta carotene are frequently used antioxidants. Many ALS specialists recommend these substances as a method of protecting motor neurons from damage from free radicals, even though there is no scientific data to suggest that these supplements alter the course of the disease.

Some patients try taking other supplements, such as B vitamins, zinc, allopurinol, grape seed extract, and milk thistle extract. In addition, calcium, magnesium, potassium, silicon, bee pollen, flaxseed oil, salmon oil, lecithin, and coenzyme-Q are

Patients who have swallowing difficulties are advised to consume thick liquids such as fruit nectar or milkshakes rather than thin liquids like water, coffee, tea, or soda because thick liquids are less likely to get into the airway. To make soups thicker, dietitians recommend mixing them in a blender with potatoes and vegetables. Juices, water, and coffee can be made thicker with commercial thickening powder. Milkshakes are thickened by blending in fruits such as strawberries or bananas. Patients who have trouble swallowing are also advised to eat soft, moist foods that slide down the throat easily. These include things like moist meatloaf, omelets, chicken or tuna salad with extra mayonnaise, canned fruit, mashed potatoes, well-cooked vegetables, and puddings. Foods to avoid are dry, hard, sticky, or fibrous items like bread, raw fruits or vegetables, nuts, peanut butter, and crackers. Once soft, moist foods become too difficult to swallow, it may be necessary to prepare all food in a blender or food processor so it has the consistency of baby food.

frequently tried. Again, there is no scientific evidence that any of these supplements helps ALS, but doctors say that moderate amounts probably will not hurt ALS patients. Other patients try herbs such as St.-John's-wort, echinacea, garlic, goldenseal, ginseng, ginkgo, and valerian in hopes of helping their condition, but doctors warn that some of these can have serious side effects and there is no proof that they do anything positive for ALS.

The use of the amino acid creatine, a performance-enhancing supplement often used by athletes, is also currently popular with Lou Gehrig's disease patients. This is in part because research on mice with ALS shows that creatine exerts a protective effect on motor neurons, makes the mice live longer, and makes their muscles remain healthy longer than control animals. Studies on humans with ALS are needed to determine whether creatine has the same positive effects on people.

The alternative medical technique of acupuncture is also employed by some ALS patients. In this traditional Asian medical discipline, a licensed acupuncturist places tiny disposable needles at various points on the body to alleviate certain physical symptoms. Some ALS patients find that acupuncture relieves pain effectively. However, no evidence exists that this treatment changes the course or progression of ALS.

Meditation is another alternative technique that can be useful for some people with Lou Gehrig's disease. While it does not change the course of the disease, it can make patients more comfortable and relieve some of the stress associated with the illness.

Because there is no treatment for ALS that significantly alters the prognosis, many patients are willing to try just about anything that can possibly help them. Doctors emphasize, however, that any alternative therapies should be approved by the patient's neurologist in order to prevent any harmful effects. Until conventional medicine, however, comes up with treatments that are truly effective in halting or reversing the course of the disease, it is likely that affected people will continue to seek to improve their lives with methods that lie outside the realm of traditional medicine.

CHAPTER FOUR

Living with Lou Gehrig's Disease

From the time of diagnosis, living with Lou Gehrig's disease is a challenging, disheartening, and frustrating experience for the patient, family, and caregivers. People may react to the diagnosis with fear, shock, anger, denial, and a variety of other emotions. Of these, denial is very common. According to Dr. Carmel Armon in *ALS 1996 and Beyond: New Hopes and Challenges:*

> It is very hard to receive a diagnosis of ALS. The instinctive response, "It can't be true" or "Why me?" technically termed "denial" may be brief or, rarely, a permanent response. In the short term, denial may be useful by providing temporary protection from the shock of the diagnosis. However, if denial continues, it may prevent patients from becoming involved in dealing with the consequences of the diagnosis, and this may not be desirable.[15]

The shock and psychological impact of a diagnosis of ALS frequently extend beyond the patient's concern for him- or herself. It also involves worry and grieving for the family and concerns about how the family will deal with the increasing disability that inevitably goes along with ALS. The knowledge that the disease will gradually rob the patient of all muscular control and will lead to death sooner or later sometimes

ALS patients find the ongoing support of family and friends enormously comforting.

strengthens families, but often families shatter as they strive to cope with new responsibilities and stresses. Friends, too, are affected by a diagnosis of Lou Gehrig's disease and respond with a variety of emotions. Whereas some friends pull away from the patient because of shock and fear, others draw closer and try to help out.

Depression is a common response from both the patient and his or her family to the diagnosis of ALS. The depression in turn influences lifestyle and relationships for all involved, as explained in the book *Amyotrophic Lateral Sclerosis*, edited by Hiroshi Mitsumoto and Theodore L. Munsat:

Depression is a natural psychological process when one faces a serious illness such as ALS. It may affect every aspect of a person's life, including his or her personal relationships, work status, and financial status. Marital relationships and other social issues and relationships may be affected. Because physical challenges are ongoing, the situation may at times seem overwhelming.[16]

Life as the Disease Progresses

The emotions and practical lifestyle changes that patients and families face after diagnosis are often repeated time and time again as the patient's condition worsens. Just when everyone gets used to assisting the patient with dressing and bathing, for example, the person may become unable to chew or swallow and have to have a feeding tube inserted. Or, the patient may lose the ability to speak and may need to be taught to use an alternative communications device. Each time such changes occur, the grief, anger, and depression may intensify.

Moreover, the financial strain from consultations with several health professionals and for special assistive devices increases as the disease progresses. Some people have medical insurance that pays some of these costs, but many do not. Those with no insurance and no financial resources may be eligible for Medicaid or Medicare assistance. People with limited financial resources and no insurance who are not eligible for Medicaid or Medicare must often make difficult decisions about whether to pay for medication and assistive devices recommended by their doctors and other health care providers. Some simply cannot afford these things and must do without them.

Even people with medical insurance must bear other financial burdens. These may include the loss of income because the patient can no longer work, loss of income for a designated family caregiver who must give up an outside job to care for the patient, the need to pay an outside caregiver, and costs of equipment and alterations to the home not covered by insurance. Most caregivers are family members because medical insurance and Medicare do not cover the costs of hiring a caretaker for someone whose condition is not expected to improve.

Besides potentially experiencing an increasing financial drain as the disease progresses, the caregiver also faces increasing physical and emotional stress. Whereas many patients are fairly independent when first diagnosed, they grow more and more dependent on others as their symptoms worsen. This can result in extreme stress and even in burnout for the caregiver.

Linda, who cares for her ALS-afflicted daughter, Marcie, describes what it is like to be a caregiver:

> Our lives have been changed forever. She was once a very independent person and now she must rely on someone, or me for her every need. The lives of all in our family have been changed forever. We were all very independent people but now in many ways we work as one. Marcie does not go anywhere without me or her dad. I must do everything for her. I am her primary caregiver. Her dad helps in the evening and on the weekends, but there are many things that only I can do for her. My life must work around her. I cannot just "run to the store or the mall." Marcie must be willing to go with me. If she does not want to go, then I must wait till her dad gets home from work and I go at night. However, her neck is so weak now going anywhere is a challenge. We have a special headrest attached to the wheelchair that she uses in the car to hold her head. She does not like wearing it in public so that really limits us going anywhere. She can still hold her head up but the slightest movement makes her head fall forward or backwards. But we manage—you learn all kinds of little tricks when you really want to do things—like going to the mall and keeping her headrest on. We take off what is called the "halo" that holds her head to the headrest and I hold her ponytail at the back of the top of the headrest.[17]

Many caregivers feel overwhelmed by the constant and all-encompassing demands placed on them. To prevent burnout and unbearable frustration, the ALS Association offers guidance to caregivers and recommends things like taking care of oneself physically and emotionally; arranging for people such as relatives, friends, or paid help to take over the patient's care for a few hours each day; and continuing to pursue hobbies and leisure activities as much as possible. Many caregivers also

In caring for ALS patients, caregivers face ever increasing physical, emotional, and financial distress.

need professional mental health care to help them cope, and they find that it can do wonders in adjusting to the demands they face. Barbara, who cared for a husband with ALS, tells about her experience:

> On the advice of our wonderful family physician, I saw a psychiatrist and went into counseling with the psychiatrist, and so did my husband and children. Finally I took some antidepressants, which made a big difference to me because they allowed me to sort out my concerns and prioritize what was important and what wasn't important. I also had wonderful advice from a dear

friend, who said two things to me. He said, first of all, you're going to find out who your real friends are. People that you think you could count on are going to disappear, and other people are going to come from nowhere and help you out with this. And then he said, lots and lots of people are going to be taking care of your husband, but nobody is going to be taking care of you. So you're going to have to find out a way to take care of yourself. And I began to do something I'd never done before in my life, which is to go have my nails done every week, which was an

What Patients and Caregivers Say About ALS Support Groups

What do people get out of ALS support groups? Here, an individual involved with the ALS Association's Arizona chapter gives a testimonial:

First, it gives me a chance to meet other people who have ALS and their caregivers. It is good to talk with others who are in the same boat as you are. I have the opportunity to learn about and see first hand how the disease progresses in different individuals and how they are coping with their handicaps in their everyday lives.

Second, I attend to obtain valuable information from the presentations given by the ALS Association AZ Chapter staff and other professionals regarding the disease, news of research and treatment possibilities, and aids and equipment available to improve the lives of the ALS patients.

Third, and possibly most important, I attend to obtain a lift from the good-natured humor and interaction which occurs in these support group meetings . . . and I always come away from these meetings feeling much better for having had the chance to get together with old friends and make new friends with people having a common interest and a common cause.

opportunity to get in a kind of girly environment and let somebody do something for me, and it was an hour and it wasn't very expensive. So it was something I could fit in. And it did help.[18]

Support Resources

Many caregivers, patients, and families join ALS support groups to help them deal with the many issues involved in living with the disease and with caring for a person with ALS.

Another person involved with an ALS support group offers the following perspective:

I attend support group meetings because:
The coordinator makes us think through readings she brings to the meetings. Also she brings programs and speakers that help us learn how to manage the disease process. The other members that have solutions to the problems I am just beginning to face. They are also an "up" group that finds humor even while dealing with the monster, ALS. I almost always go home chuckling and more at peace with myself than before the meeting.

This ALS patient receives support from family and friends in the form of household chores and other tasks that he can no longer perform.

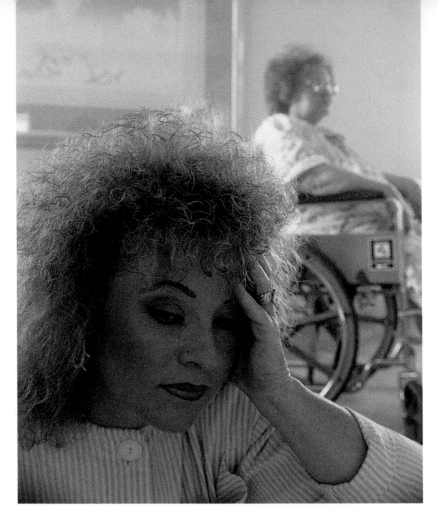

Caring for a family member with Lou Gehrig's disease can be stressful.

Support groups are made up of people going through the same thing at various stages of the disease. Such groups provide information, practical advice, and shared feelings. For many, a support group becomes the only form of social interaction since patients and their families often withdraw from other contacts as ALS progresses. This may be because of depression or because of embarrassment over declining physical functions such as the ability to speak, chew, and swallow.

Some support groups are led by a trained professional, but others are run by the participants themselves. Some allow discussion of whatever members feel like discussing; others may schedule speakers or have more formal programs. Often group members become friends and communicate outside of group meetings to offer support and encouragement.

Although ALS support groups can be sources of hope and comfort, they also can be sources of anxiety and fear as, inevitably, the members must deal with the deaths of patients in the group and confront end-of-life issues for themselves. But many who participate find them to be good sources of knowledge about Lou Gehrig's disease, its problems, and resources to turn to for help. Many also draw inspiration from patients who have managed to live fulfilling and rewarding lives despite the illness and draw solace from the feeling that they are not alone in their struggles. As pointed out by Carmel Armon in *ALS 1996 and Beyond: New Hopes and Challenges:*

> ALS may rob you of your body. It does not rob you of your soul. You live in a society that emphasizes patient autonomy. You will be able to maintain yours. While embarking on a difficult endeavor, you are not going alone. Family and friends draw closer. You will discover new friends. Other patients are available and willing to share in the ups and downs of the journey. There are many dimensions to treatment and many professionals available to provide it. The resources available to patients are without precedent.[19]

Positive Lives

Thanks to support groups, caring families and friends, dedicated professionals, and inner strength, many ALS patients manage to maintain a positive attitude and a good quality of life throughout their illness. Studies show that people with positive attitudes tend to live somewhat longer than those who are depressed and feel hopeless. The patient's family can do much to support a good quality of life by continuing to involve the person in family activities and decision making as much as possible. Patients who maintain a sense of hope and who have strong personal relationships generally have a better quality of life than those who do not.

Different patients enhance their quality of life in different ways. John, for example, coped and gave meaning to his life by practicing meditation, which enhanced his sense of self and awareness, and, despite his physical limitations, he was able to stay positive with a peaceful sense of calm until the end.

Other people with ALS find a similar sense of peace and spiritual enrichment. According to the editors of *Amyotrophic Lateral Sclerosis*, "Despite the physical decline, the lives of many people with ALS paradoxically become enriched in some ways. Typically, after initial struggles with denial and anger, they become more introspective, philosophical, caring, and tolerant. This disease, which drains one's physical strength, somehow often enables inner strength to emerge."[20]

For Dorothy, this inner strength grew from taking up painting after not attempting it for twenty years. She began creating brightly colored watercolor greeting cards that were sold to benefit the ALS Association's Michigan chapter. Says Dorothy, "I wanted to raise money for the ALS Association so that a cure can be found and others like me can be helped." When asked what her message to fellow ALS patients would be, she says, "Persevere, try not to dwell on the disease, and live each day as if it is all you have."[21]

Others afflicted with ALS derive strength and purpose from public activism. Dee found a sense of strength and self-worth by becoming an outspoken advocate for sufferers of Lou Gehrig's disease. She lobbied the U.S. Congress to increase funding for ALS research and to remove a five-month waiting period for ALS patients to receive Social Security benefits.

Another patient, Angelo, who has had ALS for more than seven years, makes life meaningful by not letting the illness stifle his spirit of adventure and through his commitment to helping others. He traveled the world photographing nature and wrote and published an inspirational book containing the photos. He donated many of the proceeds from his book to ALS fund-raisers and participated in other fund-raising and ALS awareness events as well as speaking to other patients about the disease. Says the executive director of the ALS Associa-

The ALS Association raises money for medical research. Actor Ben Stiller escorts an ALS patient at a fundraiser for a charity that supports medical research.

tion's Carolina chapter, where Angelo was a member, "Angelo's strength and courage is such an inspiration to everyone. He has proven that despite the effects of ALS, he is determined to press forward and live life to the fullest. He works so hard to support others living with ALS, not to mention other worthwhile causes like his recent campaign to send toys to the children in Iraq."[22]

Helping to support others with the disease also became a mission for Bob, who could no longer walk or speak, when he participated in a marathon to raise money for ALS. Teams of people signed up to raise funds by wheeling Bob's wheelchair for one mile of the race. When he finally crossed the finish line after 26 grueling miles (42km), the entire staff of the marathon was there to greet him with a special presentation. Remarks the president of the ALS Association's San Diego chapter:

> I'm amazed by what this man does. Bob had one of the hardest times accepting his diagnosis of anyone I had met. Yet, today he is the most cheerful, positive person in my life. He comes to all our meetings and events, reaching out to others with his unique sense of humor and always awesome smile. He is an inspiration and true friend to many people with ALS.[23]

Vicki copes with her ALS and gives her life meaning by reaching out to others with the disease in a different manner. As she wrote in an article for *Quest:*

Because ALS is incurable and steadily worsens, there is little that physicians can do for the patient as death approaches.

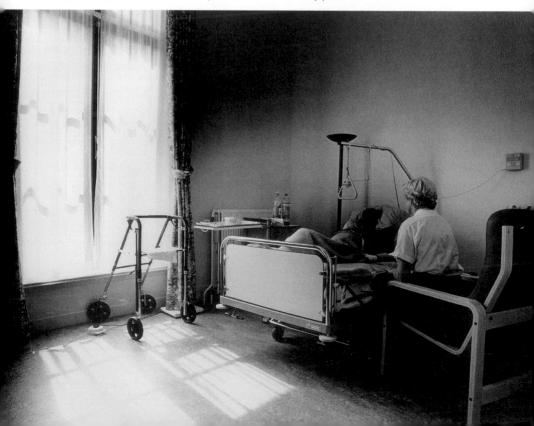

Although there's very little treatment for ALS, focusing on others is medicine for my soul. First, it reminds me there are people in the world worse off than myself. Some members of our support group have fought the ALS battle for many years. I'll never forget complaining one night about not being able to turn over in bed. One of my ALS friends, totally immobile at this point, gently reminded me to be thankful I *could* lie in bed. Discomfort and pain kept him a prisoner in his wheelchair the entire day and often at night. . . . One of the biggest benefits of focusing on others is that it gives me a safe haven for crying about the struggles of the disease and laughing in the face of terminal illness. . . . There are many practical ways to focus on others, depending on your physical limitations. The easiest of these is to share a smile or a hug. . . . Another way to push forward and not become consumed by disability is to open your home and hearts to others.[24]

End-of-Life Issues

No matter how positive ALS patients manage to be, their condition inexorably worsens. Experts recommend that patients, families, and physicians discuss legal issues related to living with ALS early on in the disease before a crisis situation arises. This way, even if the patient is unable to communicate his or her wishes, all involved will be aware of what the patient wants done when various emergencies occur. Often these preferences are formalized in legal documents known as advance directives, medical directives, or living wills. Some people sign a health care power of attorney that allows a spouse or other person to make decisions about their care.

With a terminal illness like Lou Gehrig's disease, questions of physician-assisted suicide and euthanasia may also arise. Physician-assisted suicide occurs when a patient with no hope of recovery requests that a physician prescribe a lethal drug for the patient to self-administer. Euthanasia is when a doctor administers such a drug. Although euthanasia is not legal in the United States, some doctors are willing to quietly end a patient's suffering in this way. Euthanasia is legal and is routinely practiced in some countries.

Hospice

Toward the end of their lives many ALS patients elect to receive care at a hospice facility or from hospice workers at home. This care is specially designed for patients who have less than six months to live.

Hospice care first was introduced to the United States in the 1970s. Since that time, the number and variety of hospice facilities has grown tremendously. All, however, share the same basic philosophy, which is, based on the National Hospice Organization Standards:

Dying is a normal process, whether or not resulting from disease. Hospice exists neither to hasten nor to postpone death. Rather, hospice exists to affirm life by providing support and care for those in the last phases of incurable disease so that they can live as fully and comfortably as possible. Hospice promotes the formation of caring communities that are sensitive to the needs of patients and families at this time in their lives so that they may be free to obtain the degree of mental and spiritual preparation for death that is satisfactory to them.

Because of the widespread use of hospice care, Medicare and Medicaid programs now provide benefits for patients who receive care

The U.S. Supreme Court ruled in 1997 that individual states may regulate physician-assisted suicide. The state of Oregon has since passed a law allowing this practice under certain conditions. The patient must be evaluated by more than one doctor, there must be a waiting period before the suicide is carried out, and other conditions must be met to ensure that the patient's true wishes are being upheld in a responsible manner. Since this law was enacted, several ALS patients have taken their own lives. There is a great deal of controversy about this law and about the idea of physician-assisted suicide and euthanasia in general. Some people see these practices as compassionate, but others hold the view that any life, even one in which the individual is suffering, is worth preserving.

from certain certified hospice programs. Hospice care includes nursing services, a physician who works with the patient's primary care physician, social workers for emotional support, chaplains, and volunteers who help with whatever the patient and family need. Most hospice programs also provide follow-up bereavement support for the family after the patient has died.

As they near the end of their lives, many ALS patients choose hospice care, which often allows them to die in the comfort of home.

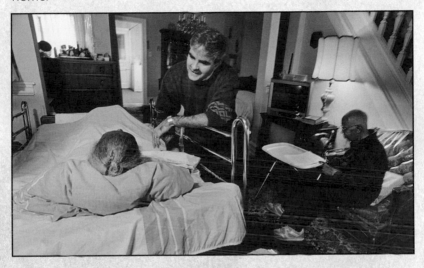

Issues of euthanasia and physician-assisted suicide aside, a patient's wish not to receive artificial life support as stated in an advance directive is a legal and widely used method of letting nature take its course in the case of a lethal disease such as ALS. At that point, making the remaining days as comfortable as possible becomes the goal. Some patients and families elect to keep the person at home and to care for him or her around the clock. Other patients enter a nursing home or hospice. A hospice is designed to provide care and support for people in the last stages of an incurable disease. Sometimes hospice care workers can come to the patient's home to administer care. Physicians, nurses, social workers, and often clergy are all involved in hospice care.

Whether the ALS patient elects to die at home or elsewhere, this is a very stressful time for all involved, and the only comfort that many derive is the knowledge that the end will be as peaceful as possible. Caregivers, family, and patients often must also learn to let go of any expectations and demands as death nears. As nurse Ann Kuckelman Cobb writes in the book *Amyotrophic Lateral Sclerosis:*

> As the disease progresses, the person with ALS may need to be given permission to simply "be" and may need assurance that his value as a human being is not tied to what he is able to do. This may be difficult because Americans share the value of the work ethic, but recognizing it as a significant influence can assist in reevaluating how it is expressed and managed. At the end, people with ALS also may need to be given permission to give up. Again, American culture values the "fighter," the one who does not give in to adversity, and people sometimes feel that they are letting everyone down when they finally feel the need to succumb. They need assurance that it is acceptable to let go.[25]

CHAPTER FIVE

The Future

Although research has thus far yielded little progress toward effectively understanding and treating Lou Gehrig's disease, a current plethora of studies makes the future look brighter all the time. Until recently, the development of new treatments for neurological diseases in general has lagged behind other fields of medicine such as cancer and AIDS (acquired immune deficiency syndrome) research. This is partly because neurology research has more often emphasized diagnosis rather than treatment. But nowadays many studies and clinical trials examine drugs and other therapies to treat neurological diseases.

Despite this shift in focus to potential treatments, however, it is unlikely that a single miracle cure for the disease will be found in the near future. According to Dr. Theodore L. Munsat in *Amyotrophic Lateral Sclerosis:*

> Rather, we most likely will be identifying drugs that have a modest slowing effect on the course of motor nerve damage such that the benefit may not be apparent to either the patient or the treating physician. This has been the case with riluzole, the first and, to date, the only drug that has been shown to slow the neurologic damage in ALS and the only drug to be approved by the U.S. Food and Drug Administration (FDA) for the treatment of ALS.[26]

Once several drugs with modest positive effects are discovered, it may then be possible to combine them into a "cocktail" that would be far more effective in treating the disease than each drug alone.

The Testing of New Drugs

Currently, several drugs are in various phases of testing for ALS. New drugs are originally invented and tested on animals in a laboratory. Once a compound has been proven to be safe and effective in a laboratory setting, the drug developer may apply to the FDA in the United States or to comparable agencies in other countries to begin testing on humans in clinical trials. A clinical trial generally involves three phases. Phase 1 lasts several months and is designed to determine safe doses and methods of taking the drug and to track any adverse effects that may occur. For example, in Phase 1 doctors determine whether the drug should be given by mouth or by injection. Only a few patients, seldom more than twenty, participate in Phase 1 trials. All are volunteers who are informed that the drug being tested may or may not help them. People volunteer for clinical trials through physicians participating in the study or by contacting research centers that advertise the trials online or through support groups aimed at patients with various diseases.

When Phase 1 trials show that a new drug appears to help people and to be without dangerous side effects, Phase 2 may begin. Here, more volunteer patients, perhaps as many as one hundred, are given the new drug to further test its safety and effectiveness. If carefully analyzed test results indicate that the drug is extremely safe and effective, the manufacturer may apply to the FDA for so-called fast-track testing status so that the medication can be made available promptly for widespread Phase 3 testing. If, on the other hand, questions remain as to whether the drug is indeed safe and worthwhile for the purpose it was developed, it may be sent back to the laboratory for modification or simply dropped from further trials.

In Phase 3, which can last several years, hundreds or even thousands of volunteers are randomly assigned to either experimental or control groups to test the drug's effectiveness. Patients in a control group are unknowingly given a placebo, or fake drug that looks like the real thing. This control is necessary because sometimes volunteers who receive the placebo in clinical trials experience positive effects simply because they hope and expect to be helped. Thus, if results from the control and experimental groups are very similar, scientists cannot rule out the possibility that expectations that the new drug will work, rather than the drug itself, are responsible for any perceived healing. If, on the other hand, researchers determine that a sufficient number of people in the experimental group show marked improvement compared with those in the placebo group, doctors can attribute the positive results to the medication.

Once Phase 3 is completed satisfactorily, the FDA may approve the new drug for marketing, and doctors may begin prescribing the drug for patients not included in the trials. Sometimes drug manufacturers then conduct Phase 4 studies that follow the drug's safety and effectiveness over many years.

Several new drugs for Lou Gehrig's disease are being developed by pharmaceutical companies.

New Drugs Being Tested

Among the drugs being tested for ALS is ceftriaxone, currently used as an antibiotic. This drug affects the neurotransmitter glutamate by activating the gene for the protein EAAT2, which results in this protein properly balancing the level of glutamate in the brain. Once the level of glutamate is reduced, neuron death is also reduced. Ceftriaxone was recently found to prolong survival in rats with ALS. Researchers are now beginning human clinical trials with the drug. Since this medication is already approved to treat humans for infections, it can be approved for clinical trials for another purpose sooner than it would be if it were an entirely new drug.

The experimental drug Copaxone has increased survival rates of mice with ALS.

Another drug being tested on ALS patients is glatiramer acetate, brand name Copaxone, currently used to treat multiple sclerosis and shown to protect neurons in a recent study involving Parkinson's disease. This medication has also been shown to increase survival in mice with ALS. It works by slowing inflammation in the brain and by increasing growth-factor production surrounding neurons.

A study by researchers at Brigham and Women's Hospital in Boston found that ALS mice treated with a combination of the drugs creatine and minocycline survived longer than those treated with either drug alone. The scientists hope to test this combination on humans with ALS. Both drugs are already approved for use for other conditions and have few adverse effects, so doctors are optimistic that the combination can be approved quickly for use in the treatment of human ALS if it is effective.

Some researchers are testing drugs to treat specific symptoms of ALS. For example, investigators have begun clinical trials to see if a drug called neurodex is effective in treating the inappropriate or uncontrollable emotional outbursts that affect some ALS patients.

One area of drug investigation centers on stopping the clumping of the SOD1 protein in the nervous system. When the SOD1 gene is mutated, it has been found to cause the SOD1 protein to clump, and this process at least partly underlies the development of Lou Gehrig's disease. Researchers have found several compounds that inhibit SOD1 clumping in laboratory test tubes. Investigators at the Harvard Center for Neurodegeneration and Repair in Boston are planning to begin testing some of the compounds on mice with ALS.

One problem with all testing of drugs against ALS is the lack of a simple test that can be done to gauge the effectiveness of a particular drug. For many diseases there are clearly defined markers, such as a blood test, that can show positive or negative effects of a treatment. But with ALS, markers of success are not as easy to measure. Currently, doctors use muscle strength, breathing capacity, and length of survival as markers, but they are hoping to develop simpler measurements. Several

researchers looking for biomarkers for ALS are now conducting studies to test for substances in the blood or cerebrospinal
fluid that could be measured to assess the effectiveness of a
treatment. Recently Dr. Robert Bowser of the University of
Pittsburgh School of Medicine discovered a group of protein
biomarkers that can be used to help diagnose ALS. He has developed a test that analyzes a drop of cerebrospinal fluid for
certain proteins linked to the disease. Some day this test may be
used to measure treatment success as well as aid in diagnosis.

Research into Neuron Growth Factors

Besides developing and testing new drugs, researchers are also
exploring the use of growth factors, which cause cells to grow
and sometimes to repair themselves, to encourage the regener-
ation of neurons. Scientists once thought that it was impossible for mature neurons to repair themselves or regrow, but
recent evidence suggests otherwise. Harnessing this mecha-
nism by manipulating neuron growth factors or similar chemicals might lead to treatments for nerve disorders like Lou
Gehrig's disease.

Recent research on growth factors has centered on several
compounds. In one study, a team of Belgian researchers found
that infusion of VEGF into the fluid surrounding the brains and
spinal cords of rats with ALS increased the animals' survival
time by about twenty days and improved motor skills. The investigators believe this is because VEGF helps motor neurons
to repair or regrow.

Other studies in the United States focus on insulin-like
growth factor 1 (IGF-1). Once IGF-1 is introduced into the
nervous system, it induces neurons to grow axons and blocks
the chemical reactions inside neurons that cause these cells
to die. Previous efforts to deliver IGF-1 and similar compounds to the nervous system failed, but a new approach in
which this chemical was attached to a harmless virus that
naturally infects neurons was successful in mice. Researchers hope to begin testing this method of administration
on humans with ALS.

Project ALS

One of the leaders in ALS research is Project ALS, an organization founded to develop new treatments and a cure for the disease. Project ALS began in 1998 as a result of efforts by Jenifer Estess, a thirty-five-year-old theater and film producer who was diagnosed with ALS. When she realized that there were no coordinated programs established to understand and develop treatments for Lou Gehrig's disease, Estess, along with her sister and friends, began Project ALS to organize such an endeavor. Since that time, Project ALS has raised more than $20 million and has funded numerous research projects to study the causes and treatments of this devastating disease. The organization accepts project proposals from researchers all over the world and seeks out prominent ALS investigators to collaborate on important projects of interest.

Project ALS research focuses on several important areas. One area is genetics. Current projects work to identify genes linked to ALS and to manipulate genes to treat ALS. Another major area of research involves stimulating stem cells to grow into motor neurons and transplanting these cells into ALS patients as a method of treating or curing the disease. A third area of research is developing new drugs to treat ALS and testing drugs approved for other diseases on Lou Gehrig's disease. A fourth is looking at the causes of ALS on a cellular level, within the body, and with respect to external factors that may play a role.

Investigators are also testing other growth factors to see how they interact with different receptors on neurons. In order for these growth factors to work, they must bind to receptors on the cells. Once researchers determine to which receptors the growth factors bind, they can then try to protect specific motor neurons with specific growth factors.

Stem Cell Research

Another new area of research involves stem cells. Stem cells are cells that have the potential to develop into many different

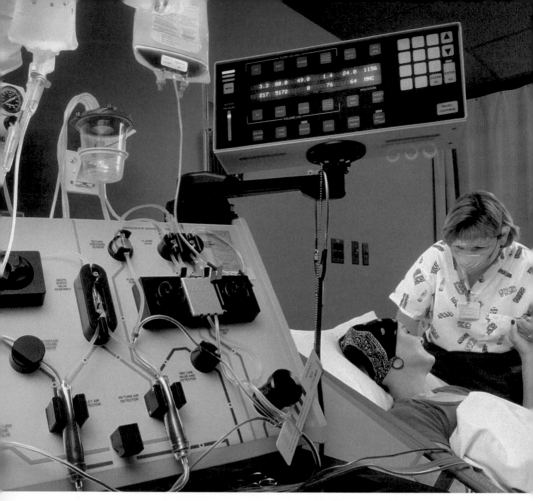

Stem cells are collected from adults and then grown in a laboratory in a process called apheresis.

cell types in the body. Researchers work with two kinds of stem cells from animals and humans: embryonic stem cells and adult stem cells. Embryonic stem cells are taken from embryos created in a laboratory. Adult stem cells are found in adult humans or animals and can be taken out to then grow in a laboratory to be used as replacements for diseased cells. When a stem cell grows and divides, each new cell can become another type of cell depending on directions the stem cell receives from certain chemicals in the body or in a laboratory. Under experimental conditions, stem cells can be prompted to become cells with special functions. Scientists have discovered that stem cells can be induced to grow into neurons that function normally. If techniques for growing and transplanting stem cells can be perfected, this could lead to possibilities for reversing or even curing ALS.

Researchers at the University of Wisconsin found that stem cells' maturation into a particular type of cell is determined by molecules that direct the stem cell early in its life. The molecule that directs stem cells to become motor neurons is called sonic hedgehog. It is stimulated by a chemical called retinoic acid. Together these two compounds enable a stem cell to become a fully functioning motor neuron. The researchers used these compounds to induce stem cells to mature into motor neurons in a laboratory. They then grafted these motor neurons into the spinal cord of chick embryos to see whether they would migrate to the proper place for making connections with developing limbs and muscle fibers. The cells did in fact proceed to the desired location in the spinal cord and then grew axons to connect with appropriate arms, legs, and muscle cells. The next step in this research will be to develop a method of transplanting stem cell–derived motor neurons into mice with ALS to see if the cells improve their condition. The investigators believe that knowledge of this process will potentially be useful in treating motor neuron diseases in the future by using the motor neurons to replace those that are lost. Comments Dr. Lucie Bruijn, "The ability to produce human motor neurons in lab dishes is of immense value, not only for future therapy, but immediately, as a research tool to learn about new targets for motor neuron disease."[27]

While most research with stem cells uses cells taken from embryos, one study used stem cells that were taken from the brains of healthy adult mice and transplanted into the spinal cords of mice with ALS. This resulted in fully functioning motor neurons that prolonged the animals' lives and delayed the progress of motor symptoms. The investigators plan to do further research to find out if the progression of ALS will damage the newly grown neurons.

Other recent research has found that non-neuronal cells that surround motor neurons can also play a role in protecting or

damaging the motor neuron cells in mice. This means that replacing the surrounding cells with stem cells is also a possible
method of prolonging survival in ALS. Says Dr. Don Cleveland,
lead author of this study:

> We've been given a new principle for extending, or perhaps
> overcoming ALS, based on how many healthy cells surround an
> ailing motor nerve cell. We're seeing a real-life metaphor, living

The Controversy over Stem Cell Research

Research progress involving stem cells, which have the potential to
replace motor neurons in cases of Lou Gehrig's disease and to replace
other types of cells in other diseases, has been slow because the sub-
ject has become a political as well as a scientific issue. On August 9,
2001, President George W. Bush signed legislation restricting federal
funding of stem cell research to stem cell lines already taken from human embryos. Behind this legislation was the belief of Bush and some
who share his political ideologies that taking stem cells from embryos
destroys a life, because otherwise the embryo would have the potential to mature into a human baby. Opponents of this view believe that
the potential for curing many devastating illnesses with stem cells
outweighs the disadvantages of destroying embryos that would have
been destroyed anyway. Embryos used in stem cell research are extras
made and stored in a laboratory for use in impregnating infertile
women. Since they are extras, however, they would simply be destroyed if they were not used as sources of stem cells.

The current legislation does not restrict funding for stem cells
taken from adults, but experts say that adult stem cells do not have
the potential to differentiate into any type of cell as do embryonic
stem cells. This has led many scientists and advocates of embryonic
stem cell research to argue that the Bush administration policy

in a bad environment can damage good cells. More importantly, restoring a better environment to "bad" neurons by surrounding them with healthy neighbors can significantly lessen toxic effects. In some cases, having normal cells completely stops motor neuron death.[28]

The investigators believe that the healthy non-neuronal cells protect motor neurons by nourishing them and by scavenging

should be changed. Among those who have publicly advocated support for embryonic stem cell research are actor Christopher Reeve (now deceased), who suffered from a spinal cord injury; actor Michael J. Fox, who has Parkinson's disease; former first lady Nancy Reagan, whose husband, former president Ronald Reagan, died from Alzheimer's disease; and Senate majority leader Bill Frist, a conservative who previously supported the Bush administration policy but spoke out in support of embryonic stem cell research in August 2005. On the other side of the issue are many antiabortion advocates and lawmakers, who equate using embryos to obtain stem cells with aborting a fetus from a woman's womb.

A scientist studies colonies of embryonic stem cells. Some people believe that stem cell research may lead to a cure for ALS.

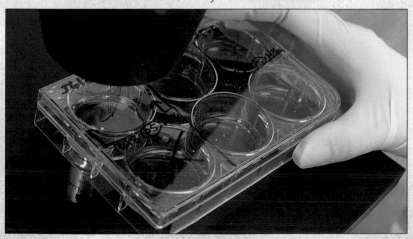

environmental toxins. When these cells become unhealthy due to damage from the mutant SOD1 gene that is found in the cells of mice with ALS, they can no longer protect motor neurons and the motor neurons die. Further research on this topic is planned to fully determine how well replacing unhealthy non-neuronal cells with stem cells will work and to see if this process is easier than replacing motor neurons with stem cells.

New Technology Is Undergoing Testing

While much ALS research involves techniques for possibly reversing or curing the disease, there are also investigations centered on improving the quality of life for patients through revolutionary new technologies. One such technology is an implantable computer chip called the Brain Gate. Invented by Cyberkinetics Neurotechnology Systems, the Brain Gate is implanted in the part of the brain that controls movement. The chip senses brain cell activity and relays the information to a small pedestal placed on the head and connected to the chip with a thin wire. The pedestal is in turn connected by a cable to a cart containing computers, signal processors, and monitors. The goal is for the patient's thoughts to be converted to commands by the signal processors and for these commands to then be fed to a computer and used to control the movement of the computer cursor. Scientists can observe the process using the computers, signal processors, and monitors set up beside the patient.

Using the patient's thoughts to control a computer cursor would give many people paralyzed by ALS the ability to use a computer and perhaps more in the future.

> If study participants are able to gain control over a computer cursor with the BrainGate System, this could open the door to controlling a broad range of other devices, including assistive communication devices, speech synthesizers, and, eventually, devices to re-enable limb movement. Furthermore, by recording neural activity over time in participants with ALS, this study may help to provide additional insights into the neurodegenerative process that occurs with this complex disease.[29]

says Dr. Leigh R. Hochberg of Massachusetts General Hospital, the principal investigator of a new study to test the Brain Gate in ALS patients. This study was initiated in August 2005. Prior to this investigation, researchers conducted tests of the new technology on patients with spinal cord injuries and reported positive results.

Researchers working with ALS patients are testing an implant like this, which allows this quadriplegic to control a computer with his thoughts.

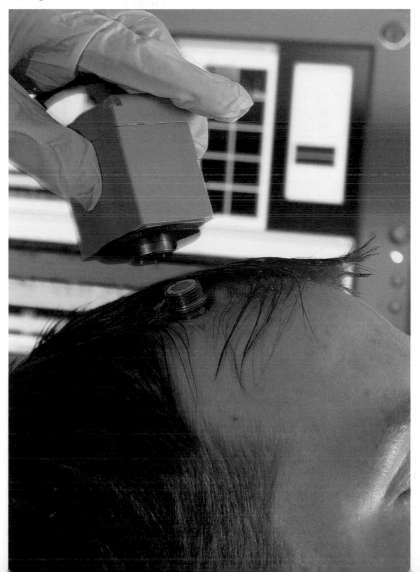

Research into the Genetic Causes of ALS

Another area of current and future research is exploring the causes of Lou Gehrig's disease. One important concern is the search for genes other than the SOD1 gene mutation that may play a role in causing the disease. Scientists have discovered that several genes on chromosomes sixteen, eighteen, and twenty are potential candidates. Once certain gene mutations are conclusively linked to ALS, there exists the possibility of using gene therapy to correct the mutations. Gene therapy currently uses several experimental techniques for correcting

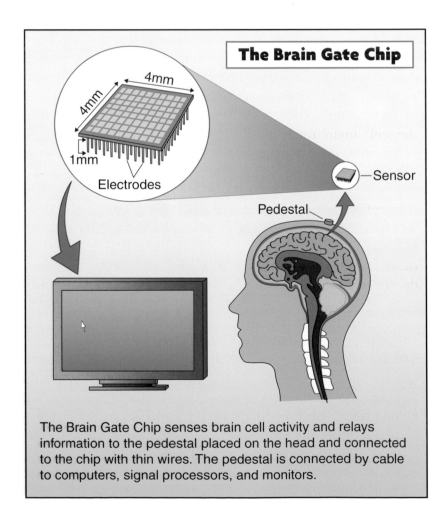

The Brain Gate Chip senses brain cell activity and relays information to the pedestal placed on the head and connected to the chip with thin wires. The pedestal is connected by cable to computers, signal processors, and monitors.

faulty genes. The most common technique involves inserting a normal gene into a cell to replace a mutated gene. This normal gene is delivered to the patient's target cells using a carrier molecule known as a vector. The most common type of vector used is a virus that has been genetically altered so that it is incapable of causing an infection. Because viruses are adept at entering and delivering genetic material to living cells, the theory behind using them as vectors is that they can be attached to replacement genes and then released into the desired area (for example, into the brain). Once the vector gets the replacement gene into the correct cells, the gene can start functioning normally to correct the deficiency caused by a mutated gene.

Besides using vectors to insert normal genes into cells, scientists are also experimenting with other methods of getting these genes into their targets. These methods include directly placing the gene inside a cell, linking DNA to molecules that bind to cell receptors and then pass through the cell membrane, and introducing an artificial chromosome containing certain genes into the nucleus of a target cell. None of these techniques has yet been perfected.

In addition to replacing a mutated gene with a normal one, researchers are exploring other methods of correcting faulty genes. One technique involves repairing a disease-causing gene through a process called selective reverse mutation, which returns the gene to its normal function. Another is altering the degree to which a particular gene is turned on or off. A third is using a method known as homologous recombination to swap an abnormal gene for a normal one.

Once a normal gene is successfully placed into an appropriate cell, researchers must ensure that it remains functional for a long time so that it will be an effective cure for the disease. This is another challenge facing gene therapy as a long-term solution to problems brought on by mutated genes. Another potential factor that could limit the effectiveness of gene therapy is an immune system response by the body. Any time a foreign object is introduced into human or animal tissue, the immune system attacks the invader. If the immune system attacks the replacement gene, this could render the gene incapable of functioning.

Thus far, none of the gene therapy techniques has been developed to the degree necessary for using them to cure diseases. Several clinical trials using vector-carried genes have been attempted, but the results have been mixed. The science of gene therapy suffered a huge setback in 1999, when eighteen-year-old Jesse Gelsinger died during a gene therapy trial at the University of Pennsylvania. Then, in 2003, several children in a French gene therapy trial developed leukemia. Since these incidents, trials involving gene therapy have been proceeding cautiously and progress has been slow. However, investigators are continuing with research along these lines because of the immense potential gene therapy shows for curing a variety of diseases.

In March 2005 investigators conducting other research on genes discovered a way to interrupt the genetic instructions for making the SOD1 gene in mice. This led to improved motor skills and survival. Says Bruijn, "These studies are extremely exciting and provide a promising approach to treat familial forms of ALS linked to mutations in SOD1. As we learn more about the other genes involved in the disease a similar approach can be taken for those forms of ALS not linked to the SOD1 mutation."[30]

Other Research on Causes

Also dealing with the causes of ALS is a study of the prevalence of the disease in areas near hazardous waste sites in five states, conducted by investigators with the Agency for Toxic Substances and Disease Registry, a public health agency of the U.S. Department of Health and Human Services. This study may help determine what sorts of environmental toxins contribute to the development of ALS. If Lou Gehrig's disease is more prevalent than usual in these areas, then the researchers will try to determine which toxic substances are present and how those substances may cause ALS. If there are not higher than usual rates of the disease in these locations, the toxic compounds in question are probably not associated with ALS.

Delineating the causes of Lou Gehrig's disease was also the goal of recent research on mice, which revealed that the illness may be related to problems with mitochondria, the energy factories of cells. Investigators in a French study at the National Center for Scientific Research in Paris found that mitochondrial malfunctions in nerve cells and in skeletal muscle cells led to a failure to effectively turn food into energy in both types of cells. Without enough energy to keep working properly, the cells degenerated, leading to symptoms of ALS. Feeding the mice a diet high in fat and energy appeared to reduce the loss of nerve and muscle cells and to prolong survival time. But before recommending such a dietary change in humans with ALS, experts say more research is needed. "This was a laboratory study using a mouse model. We have to be very careful before

Scientists believe that gene therapy may one day be used to treat ALS patients.

we make a diet change in people. It could be harmful, because in many patients a careful balance is needed,"[31] says Bruijn.

Hope for the Future

The goal of all ALS research, whether it involves causes or treatments, is to develop effective therapies and eventually to find a cure for the disease. Although these innovations may still be far in the future, experts see reason for hope because of the current research that is being conducted. According to the ALS Association:

> More significant advances of research into ALS has occurred in the last decade than all of the time since Charcot identified the disease. Advances in technology and the genetic revolution are aiding researchers in unlocking the ALS mystery. As more scientists focus on this perplexing disease, the outlook for new understanding brightens each day.[32]

Notes

Introduction: Who Was Lou Gehrig?

1. Quoted in Lou Gehrig Official Web Site, Farewell Speech. www.lougehrig.com/about/speech.htm.
2. Lou Gehrig Official Web Site, "Biography." www. lougehrig.com/about/bio.htm.

Chapter 1: What Is Lou Gehrig's Disease?

3. Hiroshi Mitsumoto and Theodore L. Munsat, eds., *Amyotrophic Lateral Sclerosis*. New York: Demos, 2001, p. 26.
4. Muscular Dystrophy Association, "Facts About Amyotrophic Lateral Sclerosis (ALS)." www.mdausa.org/publications/fa-als.html.
5. ALS Association, "Diagnosing ALS." www.alsa.org/als/diagnosing.cfm?CFID=481551&CFTOKEN=83307959.
6. Mitsumoto and Munsat, eds., *Amyotrophic Lateral Sclerosis*, p. 201.

Chapter 2: What Causes Lou Gehrig's Disease?

7. Muscular Dystrophy Association, "Facts About Amytrophic Lateral Sclerosis (ALS)."
8. Quoted in ALS Association, "Scientists Announce Two New Genetic Sites Linked to Familial ALS." www.alsa.org/news/article.cfm?id=241&CFID=481551&CFTOKEN=83307959.
9. Quoted in Project ALS, "New Evidence of Retroviral Involvement in Amyotrophic Lateral Sclerosis." www.projectals.org/researchnews.shtml.
10. Quoted in ALS Association, "New Research Involving Gulf War Veterans Could Provide Insight About ALS." www.alsa.org/news/article.cfm?id=2398CFID=481551&CFTOKEN=83307959.

11. Quoted in ALS Association, "Military Veterans at Greater Risk of ALS/Lou Gehrig's Disease New ALSA Report Shows." www.alsa.org/news/article.cfm?id=644.

Chapter 3:
How Is Lou Gehrig's Disease Treated?

12. Dan Stimson, "Exercise Has Many Benefits for People with ALS," *MDA/ALS Newsletter*, October 2002. www.mdausa. org/publications/als/als7_8.html#alslive.
13. Muscular Dystrophy Association, "Facts About Amyotrophic Lateral Sclerosis (ALS)."
14. Quoted in ALS Association, "Tips for Newly Diagnosed ALS Patients from Will Hubben." www.alsa.org/community/ article.cfm?id=383&CFID=481551&CFTOKEN=83307959.

Chapter 4:
Living with Lou Gehrig's Disease

15. Carmel Armon, *ALS 1996 and Beyond: New Hopes and Challenges*. www.llu.edu/llumc/neurosciences/als/#what.
16. Mitsumoto and Munsat, eds., *Amyotrophic Lateral Sclerosis*, p. 72.
17. Quoted in ALS Association, "Interview with Linda Gibson." www.alsa.org/community/article.cfm?id=437&CFID= 481551&CFTOKEN=83307959.
18. Quoted in ALS Association, "Messages from Barbara Dickinson." www.alsa.org/patient/dickinson2.cfm?CFID= 481551 &CFTOKEN=83307959.
19. Armon, *ALS 1996 and Beyond*.
20. Mitsumoto and Munsat, eds., *Amyotrophic Lateral Sclerosis*, p. 278.
21. Quoted in ALS Association, "Dorothy Wood: Regained Artist's Touch After Developing ALS." www.alsa.org/com munity/article.cfm?id=567&CFID=481551&CFTOKEN= 83307959.
22. Quoted in ALS Association, "Angelo Sciulli: Giving ALS One Big Shiner." www.alsa.org/community/article.cfm? id=534&CFID=481551&CFTOKEN=83307959.
23. Quoted in ALS Association, "Stories of Courage: Bob

Dennis." www.alsa.org/community/article.cfm?id=265&
CFID= 481551&CFTOKEN=83307959.

24. Vicki Wolff, "Focusing on Others Helps Oneself," *Quest*,
January/February 2005. www.mdausa.org/publications/
Quest/q121fromwhere.cfm.

25. Quoted in Mitsumoto and Munsat, eds., *Amyotrophic
Lateral Sclerosis*, p. 244.

Chapter 5: The Future

26. Mitsumoto and Munsat, eds., *Amytrophic Lateral Sclerosis*, p. 212.

27. Quoted in ALS Association, "Details Discovered on How
Human Stem Cells Become Nerve Cells." www.alsa.org/
news/article.cfm?id=581&CFID=481551&CFTOKEN=
83307959.

28. Quoted in ALS Association, "Healthy Non-neuronal Cells
Extend Survival of Motor Neurons in Mouse Model; Study
Holds Promise for Stem Cell Therapy for ALS Patients."
www.alsa.org/news/article.cfm?id=2368&CFID=481551&C
FTOKEN=83307959.

29. Quoted in "ALS Patients Offered Access to Cyberkinetics'
BrainGate System in New Pilot Study at Massachusetts
General Hospital." http://biz.yahoo.com/bw/
0508221225405.html?.v=1.

30. Quoted in ALS Association, "New Gene Silencing Technique Promising in Animal Studies Funded by the ALS Association." www.alsa.org/news/article.cfm?id=613.

31. Quoted in Health Day, "New Clues to Cause of Lou
Gehrig's Disease." www.healthday.com/view.cfm?id=
520125.

32. ALS Association, "About ALS." www.alsa.org/als/
default.cfm?CFID=481551&CFTOKEN=83307959.

Glossary

amyotrophic lateral sclerosis: A progressive degenerative disease marked by destruction of nerve cells that control voluntary muscle movement.

antioxidant: A chemical compound that inhibits oxidation.

atrophy: Muscle wasting.

axon: A long extension of a nerve cell that carries messages to the next nerve cell.

bulbar: Concerning the facial muscles, speech, and swallowing.

central nervous system: The brain and spinal cord.

cerebrospinal fluid: The liquid that flows within the cavities of the brain and around the brain and spinal cord.

chromosome: The wormlike body on which genes are located in the nucleus of each cell.

dendrite: Extensions on a nerve cell that receive information from neighboring nerve cells.

familial ALS: A form of ALS that is inherited.

free radical: A chemical that is highly reactive and can oxidize and damage other molecules.

gene: The part of a DNA molecule that transmits hereditary information.

glutamate: An excitatory neurotransmitter whose excesses are thought to be responsible for neuronal damage in ALS.

mutation: A change in genetic material.

neurological: Pertaining to the nervous system.

neuron: A nerve cell.

neurotransmitter: A brain chemical involved in communication between nerve cells.

sporadic ALS: A form of ALS that is not inherited.

superoxide dismutase: An enzyme that normally destroys free radicals.

synapse: The junction between two nerve cells.

Organizations to Contact

ALS Association

National Office, 27001 Agoura Rd., Suite 150, Calabasas Hills, CA 91301-5104

(800) 782-4747

www.alsa.org

The ALS Association provides information, support, and research to ALS patients and families.

American Academy of Neurology (AAN)

2221 University Ave. SE, Suite 335, Minneapolis, MN 55414

(651) 695-1940

www.aan.com

The AAN provides information on many neurological diseases, including ALS.

Muscular Dystrophy Association (MDA)

National Office, 3300 East Sunrise Dr., Tucson, AZ 85718-3208

(520) 529-2000

www.mdausa.org

The MDA provides information and referrals on forty neuromuscular diseases, including ALS.

Project ALS

900 Broadway, Suite 901, New York, NY 10003

(800) 603-0270

www.projectALS.org

Project ALS discusses research news and seeks to raise awareness of ALS.

For Further Reading

Books

Robert Miller, Patricia O'Connor, and Deborah Gelinas, *Amyotrophic Lateral Sclerosis*. New York: Demos Medical, 2004. Covers all aspects of ALS and living with the disease.

Mary Dodson Wade, *ALS: Lou Gehrig's Disease*. Berkeley Heights, NJ: Enslow, 2001. Discusses the disease, treatment, research, and case studies.

Periodical

Marianne Szegedy-Maszak, "A Gulf War Legacy," *U.S. News & World Report*, December 24, 2001.

Works Consulted

Books

Hiroshi Mitsumoto and Theodore L. Munsat, eds., *Amyotrophic Lateral Sclerosis*. New York: Demos, 2001. A comprehensive book on ALS and living with the disease.

Internet Sources

ALS Association, "About ALS." www.alsa.org/als/default.cfm? CFID=481551&CFTOKEN=83307959.

———, "ALS Prevalence Studies Underway Near Hazardous Waste Sites." www.alsa.org/news/article.cfm?id=441&CFID =481551&CFTOKEN=83307959.

———, "Angelo Sciulli: Giving ALS One Big Shiner." www. alsa.org/community/article.cfm?id=534&CFID=481551&CF TOKEN=83307959.

———, "Details Discovered on How Human Stem Cells Become Nerve Cells." www.alsa.org/news/article.cfm?id=581& CFID=481551&CFTOKEN=83307959.

———, "Diagnosing ALS." www.alsa.org/als/diagnosing.cfm? CFID=481551&CFTOKEN=83307959.

———, "Dorothy Wood: Regained Artist's Touch After Developing ALS." www.alsa.org/community/article.cfm?id=567& CFID=481551&CFTOKEN=83307959.

———, "Genetic Testing for ALS." www.alsa.org/als/genetics. cfm?CFID=481551&CFTOKEN=83307959.

———, "Healthy Non-neuronal Cells Extend Survival of Motor Neurons in Mouse Model; Study Holds Promise for Stem Cell Therapy for ALS Patients." www.alsa.org/news/ article.cfm?id=2368CFID=481551&CFTOKEN=83307959.

———, "Interview with Linda Gibson." www.alsa.org/community/article.cfm?id=437&CFID=481551&CFTOKEN= 83307959.

————, "Messages from Barbara Dickinson." www.alsa.org/patient/dickinson2.cfm?CFID=481551&CFTOKEN=83307959.

————, "Military Veterans at Greater Risk of ALS/Lou Gehrig's Disease New ALSA Report Shows." www.alsa.org/news/article.cfm?id=644.

————, "New Gene Silencing Technique Promising in Animal Studies Funded by the ALS Association." www.alsa.org/news/article.cfm?id=613.

————, "New Research Involving Gulf War Veterans Could Provide Insight About ALS." www.alsa.org/news/article.cfm?id=2398CFID=481551&CFTOKEN=83307959.

————, "Scientists Announce Two New Genetic Sites Linked to Familial ALS." www.alsa.org/news/article.cfm?id=241&CFID=481551&CFTOKEN=83307959.

————, "Stories of Courage: Bob Dennis." www.alsa.org/community/article.cfm?id=265&CFID=481551&CFTOKEN=83307959.

————, "Tips for Newly Diagnosed ALS Patients from Will Hubben." www.alsa.org/community/article.cfm?id=383&CFID=481551&CFTOKEN=83307959.

Carmel Armon, *ALS 1996 and Beyond: New Hopes and Challenges*. www.llu.edu/llume/neurosciences/als/#what.

Businesswire, "ALS Patients Offered Access to Cyberkinetics' BrainGate System in New Pilot Study at Massachusetts General Hospital." home.businesswire.com/portal/site/google/index.jsp?ndmViewId=news_view&news.

Health Day, "New Clues to Cause of Lou Gehrig's Disease." www.healthday.com/view.cfm?id=520125.

Lou Gehrig Official Web Site, "Biography." www.lougehrig.com/about/bio.htm.

————, "Farewell Speech." www.lougehrig.com/about/speech.htm.

Muscular Dystrophy Association, "Facts About Amyotrophic Lateral Sclerosis (ALS)." www.mdausa.org/publications/faals.html.

Project ALS, "New Evidence of Retroviral Involvement in Amyotrophic Lateral Sclerosis." www.projectals.org/research news.shtml.

Dan Stimson, "Exercise Has Many Benefits for People with ALS," *MDA/ALS Newsletter*, October 2002. www.mdausa. org/publications/als/als7_8.html#alslive.

Vicki Wolff, "Focusing on Others Helps Oneself," *Quest*, January/February 2005. www.mdausa.org/publications/Quest/q121fromwhere.cfm.

Index

Picture Credits

About the Author

Melissa Abramovitz grew up in San Diego, California, and as a teenager developed an interest in medical topics. She began college with the intention of becoming a doctor but later switched majors, graduating summa cum laude from the University of California, San Diego, with a degree in psychology in 1976.

Launching her career as a freelance writer in 1986 to allow herself to be an at-home mom when her two children were small, she realized she had found her niche. She continues to write regularly for magazines and educational book publishers. In her nineteen years as a freelancer she has published hundreds of articles and numerous short stories, poems, and books for children, teens, and adults. Many of her works are on medical topics.